Growing Up Roosevelt

Growing Up Roosevelt

A Granddaughter's Memoir of Eleanor Roosevelt

NINA ROOSEVELT GIBSON

EXCELSIOR
EDITIONS

Cover images: Top: The Stone Cottage at Val-Kill, Eleanor Roosevelt National Historic Site, Hyde Park, New York, USA. Photo: Acroterion, Creative Commons ShareAlike 4.4 license. Bottom: Sally, ER, Nina with Fala on leash, Tamas behind. Photo 1951, author's collection.

Author's proceeds will be donated to continue the work and legacy of Eleanor Roosevelt.

Published by State University of New York Press, Albany

Excelsior Editions is an imprint of State University of New York Press

For information, contact State University of New York Press, Albany, NY www.sunypress.edu

Library of Congress Cataloging-in-Publication Data

Name: Gibson, Nina Roosevelt, 1942– author.
Title: Growing up Roosevelt : a granddaughter's memoir of Eleanor Roosevelt / Nina Roosevelt Gibson.
Other titles: Granddaughter's memoir of Eleanor Roosevelt
Description: Albany, NY : State University of New York Press, [2023] | Series: Excelsior editions | Includes bibliographical references and index.
Identifiers: LCCN 2023002622 | ISBN 9781438495132 (hardcover : alk. paper) | ISBN 9781438495149 (ebook)
Subjects: LCSH: Roosevelt, Eleanor, 1884–1962—Anecdotes. | Roosevelt family—Anecdotes. | Roosevelt, Eleanor, 1884–1962—Homes and haunts—Anecdotes. | Presidents' spouses—United States—Biography—Anecdotes. | Grandmothers—New York (State)—Hyde Park—Biography—Anecdotes. | Gibson, Nina Roosevelt, 1942- —Childhood and youth. | Roosevelt, Eleanor, 1884–1962—Travel—Anecdotes. | Gibson, Nina Roosevelt, 1942- —Travel—Anecdotes. | Eleanor Roosevelt National Historic Site (N.Y.)—Anecdotes.
Classification: LCC E807.1.R48 G53 2023 | DDC 973.917092 [B]—dc23/eng/20230307
LC record available at https://lccn.loc.gov/2023002622

10 9 8 7 6 5 4 3 2 1

For Haven and Russell

and

in memory of Lindsay H. Luke

Contents

Illustrations

Acknowledgments

Had it not been for the extraordinary gift of life from my donor family, over twenty years ago, this book would not have been written. The love of my life, my husband, Nick, has nurtured me through life and has contributed technically and personally to this book. In my case, it took a village to keep me going, and I am forever grateful for each and every person who extended their friendship and encouragement. My classmate and longtime friend, Janet Entrup Guzzetta, and her sister, Barbara Entrup Ziti, helped me to appreciate the contributions of their parents and the Curnan family to my grandmother's everyday life. Their memories of living at Val-Kill and knowing my grandmother in a very special way has deepened my own understanding. Michael Harris has guided this work with patience, humor, and has kept me from giving up. With thoughtful guidance, he has been a part of every step along the way. My appreciation also goes to my early readers, Erica Salzman-Talbi, April Gozza, Lynn Ruggerio, Kris Klewin, Lynn Harris, Haven Luke, and Russell Luke. Your comments and reactions were so helpful. For years many people have encouraged me to write this book, among them, Suzi Kressler, Joel Engle, Sallie Seymour, Kathy Cowan, Lauren Elliott and Holley Snaith. I thank you all and sincerely appreciate that you believed in my work. My thanks also go to the archival staff at the Franklin Delano Roosevelt Library for their time and tremendous assistance. Former Director Paul Sparrow encouraged me at a time I needed it most. Alex Lubertozzi was essential in smoothing out and bringing together all parts of the book as he guided me toward publishing. Geoffrey Ward and Blanche Weisen Cook gave me the final encouragement to actually publish my memories of my grandmother. I am grateful to Richard Carlin and all those at SUNY Press for their support, expertise, and assistance throughout this process.

Introduction

When I was seven years old, my parents uprooted our family from Southern California, the only home I had ever known, and moved us across country to Hyde Park, New York. The familiar surroundings of home—my cozy bedroom, the sound of the breeze through the palm trees, and the occasional earthquake warnings—were exchanged for a loving grandmother and a piece of land that would become a part of my soul. It was at Val-Kill Farm in Hyde Park, New York, that I shared my childhood years with my remarkable grandmother, the woman who would change my life. To me she was Grandmère, but to most everyone else, she was Eleanor Roosevelt.

As I write this in 2021, important research is still being done, and wide-ranging books continue to be written about my grandmother's life. However, my experience was direct and distinctive, and I thought it would be worthwhile for me to describe her as I came to know her. Like many children, I looked up to this woman not because I knew she was famous, but because she welcomed me with kindness and treated me as a beloved granddaughter rather than a nuisance to be tolerated until I was older and more interesting. Grandmère, as we called our grandmother, took me with her on shopping trips for groceries; to listen in on sessions at the United Nations; and on trips to Campobello Island, the Roosevelt retreat at the border between Maine and New Brunswick, Canada; as well as to Europe, Israel, and Iran. We spent time walking through the woods at Val-Kill in the early mornings and working in her flower garden, and in the evenings I loved to hear her read stories. There are numerous photographs from her visits with children around the world, her arm wrapped warmly around one or several children and eyes that exuded caring. My grandmother's broad smile became known as her "toothy" grin. I experienced the warmth and love she offered firsthand.

My grandfather, President Franklin D. Roosevelt, died when I was two and a half years old, and I have little recollection of him. However, events placed my siblings and me in a close relationship with my grandmother, nourishing our understanding of her life at home.

My father, John Roosevelt, Eleanor and Franklin's youngest child, married my mother, Anne Lindsay Clark, a sparkling young socialite from Boston. While my father served in the Navy during World War II and for a few years afterward, we lived in California, but then we moved to Val-Kill, Eleanor's enclave in Hyde Park, New York, where I lived until I married in 1964 and left home.

To me, my grandmother was not the shrewd, idealistic activist involved with issues that affected the lives of those in the

Figure I.1. Christmas at the White House, 1944. *Source*: FDR Library, public domain.

Figure I.2. John Roosevelt family: Haven, Nina, Anne, John, Joan on Anne's lap, Sally, and Shep. *Source*: Photo by T. Freudy, public domain.

world who were marginalized without a voice. From the time I was seven until I was nineteen, when Grandmère died, she was simply my grandmother. She had soft skin, would read to me and sit with me while she brushed her hair before kissing me goodnight. As a child, I saw my wise, compassionate grandmother shining bright and strong. But the Grandmère I knew was not the world's Eleanor Roosevelt who made grand speeches, lobbied for civil rights, and moved political mountains. In my world she was a loving woman who had kind eyes, a high-pitched voice, hearing aids that could be turned off when she wanted quiet, and stacks of mail that she took the time to read and respond to personally.

❦

When I was very young, I thought *Roosevelt* was a common name, like *Smith*. Most of the people I knew were named Roosevelt. What I did not realize was that they were all related to me. Not until I was older—nearly an adolescent—did I begin to appreciate the roles that my grandmother and her husband Franklin had played in all of our lives.

Born in October 1884 to prosperous merchant and real estate families in New York, one would have assumed that Eleanor led a charmed life. However, no family is immune from tragic events, illnesses, and the struggles of developing into productive members of their communities. The turmoil of my grandmother's childhood could easily have resulted in a withdrawn, sad, anxious person who saw herself as a victim rather than the woman who, as Adlai Stevenson once said, "would rather light a candle than curse the darkness." By the time Eleanor was orphaned at ten she had experienced more adversity than most people face in a lifetime. When Eleanor was eight, diphtheria took the life of one of her two younger brothers, as well as her mother, Anna Roosevelt. After her mother died, it was decided that Eleanor and her surviving, eighteen-month-old brother, Hall, should live with their widowed, maternal grandmother, Mary Livingston Ludlow Hall, and her five unmarried children who were still living at home. All three young Hall women were of marriageable age and enjoying society balls, dinner parties, or any event in New York City where they might meet a potential suitor. The two Hall men were equally engaged in New York society. Without companions of her own, my grandmother only felt useful and included while attending to these giddy young women while they pampered themselves before parties or were exhausted after the festivities. Without her aunts to run errands for, Eleanor was left alone. This was a household that fluctuated between loneliness and the chaos of socially prominent young women, leaving little time or attention for two additional children. Eleanor's beloved father, Elliot, died two years later in large part due to his alcoholism, which also profoundly impacted her life.

As a teenager, my grandmother spent three years in London at a boarding school run by Marie Souvestre. This provided her with the experiences that broadened her horizon and allowed her to think she could indeed do and think things on her own. This was a pivotal time when young Eleanor lived in a safe, encouraging environment, where she developed her own thoughts based on knowledge she gained and then learned how to discuss subjects while remaining open, listening to other points of view. Learning how to critically assess issues was the beginning of her development as a broad thinker and activist.

The marriage of Eleanor Roosevelt to Franklin D. Roosevelt brought two branches of the Roosevelt family together—the Oyster Bay Roosevelts, which included her uncle, Theodore Roosevelt, the twenty-sixth president of the United States, and the Hyde Park Roosevelts. Both branches of the family had been successful in real estate, banking, and coal and railroad investments. Both branches were involved in philanthropy and had developed friendships with other well-known families in this country and abroad. Theodore and Franklin Roosevelt were bound not only by political office but held many interests in common. Both were accomplished naturalists, were knowledgeable birders, and loved the sea and naval history. On March 17, 1905, Theodore gave Eleanor, age nineteen, in marriage to Franklin. My grandmother commented that, by marrying a Roosevelt, she at least did not have to change her monogram.

At the time of her marriage, Eleanor was a shy, quiet young woman with little confidence in her ability to engage in the domestic life that was expected of her. The evolution from an insecure, withdrawn woman took place over many years with many influences and role models, which has been, and continues to be, well documented in the hundreds of works devoted to the many aspects of her public and private life. My memory of interactions with my grandmother did not occur until after FDR's death. I have focused on my own experiences of Eleanor Roosevelt—life at home with my grandmother, the people I met thanks to her, and our travels together—rather than her extraordinary accomplishments during this time.

Widowed in 1945, Eleanor Roosevelt retreated to the only place that she had ever felt was her own and the place where she could find solace. Wearing a black armband of mourning, my grandmother walked through the woods at Val-Kill with Franklin's dog Fala and busied herself with the job of settling her late husband's estate. When asked by a reporter what she planned to do next, her answer was simple and straightforward, although not true. She said, "The story is over." It may not have occurred to my grandmother that the social inequities she had focused on during her tenure as First Lady would, in this postwar era, be brought to the forefront of politics in the U.S. Her considerable political talents, which she developed over years at the side of Franklin Roosevelt, would become critically important and sought-after during the last seventeen years of her life. My grandmother never saw herself seeking a position in government, but all of her experiences converged at the time of her widowhood. She had a passionate commitment to humanitarian values and a desire to continue to be useful as war-ravaged countries began attempting to build a better world. Immediate attention was needed across Europe as thousands of displaced persons, including orphaned children from destroyed cities and towns, needed safe housing, health care, and work opportunities. The fight for civil rights and social justice took on new urgency during the late 1940s and '50s in the U.S., leading to the protests and legislation of the 1960s. With so many in need, it did not take long for Eleanor to continue her active and hectic life of travel and advocacy. She was a master politician who did not have to worry about votes, as she would never run for public office herself. The only thing Eleanor cared about was assisting her country to become the leading humanitarian democracy that the country was designed to be.

Val-Kill is often mentioned as the place where Eleanor liked to entertain family and friends and felt at home. But few people realize how special Val-Kill was for my grandmother. No longer did she live in the shadow of her mother-in-law, her husband, or

Figure I.3. Val-Kill Cottage. *Source*: FDR Library, public domain.

the scrutiny of the public; she was, finally, able to live in a house that was truly hers.

After busy days and often weeks of lecture tours, fundraising trips, representing the United States as a delegate to the United Nations, later as a member of the U.S. Association of the United Nations, and assisting grassroots organizations around the world, my grandmother often commented about how nice it was to return to Val-Kill to "be at home again." The return to Val-Kill nourished her, allowed her time for reflection, for planning and rejuvenation so that she could continue pouring her heart and soul into the needs of so many people the world over. She loved the familiar sounds and smells of Val-Kill—the quiet winters broken by the crunch of footsteps on snow or ice, the rustic scent of smoke from fireplaces in the air. Spring brought birds and blooming lilac bushes; summers were filled with the chatter of family, the smells of the freshly mown lawn and fragrant flowers in her garden, the sounds of frogs in the pond and even the mosquitoes whirring overhead. The call of the crows announced cold breezes that brought brilliantly colored leaves to the ground in the fall. Grandmère slept on her screened-in sleeping porch as often as she could to be part of the cherished sensory pleasures of Val-Kill.

Personal relationships were a cornerstone of Eleanor Roosevelt's effectiveness as a humanitarian and politician. It was in the serenity of Val-Kill that my grandmother could spend time with activists, political leaders, and young people who were just beginning to become involved with the domestic and international issues of the time. There is no doubt she invited people to try to influence their thinking, but she also wanted to listen to other points of view. The setting at Val-Kill also allowed her to lobby for help, not only with the causes she was most interested in but on occasion for a personal motive as well. C. R. Smith, head of American Airlines, visited Val-Kill for a weekend, and during dinner I was surprised when Grandmère casually lamented, so that Mr. Smith could hear her, that she was about to embark on a long trip across the country and sadly American Airlines did not have a flight that accommodated her schedule. Mr. Smith smiled and suddenly there was an American Airlines flight going to where Grandmère needed to go at exactly the time she needed to go.

My fondest memories are of being included in so many of her activities—from gardening, to attending events at the United Nations, to entertaining guests from all walks of life, from heads of state to guests with no particular distinction other than being people my grandmother cared about. I was also fortunate enough to accompany Grandmère when she traveled to places around the country, as well as to the Middle East, Europe, and Canada. It was during the years that I lived in the Stone Cottage right next to my grandmother's Val-Kill Cottage that I learned to appreciate who this revered person was in her most intimate moments.

Spending time with my grandmother allowed me to see how she interacted with people publicly as well as privately. I

Figure I.4. Stone Cottage. *Source*: FDR Library, public domain.

was also able to experience how she interacted with people of notoriety as well as everyday people, whether wealthy or poor. I realized that no matter one's status in the community, my grandmother treated each person with the same respect. This was the example that I learned without knowing I was even learning it. So much of what my grandmother meant to me has evolved as I have matured and experienced my own life. As a child I looked up to her as my kind grandmother. As a teenager I enjoyed the wonders of seeing new places, experiencing different cultures, and learning how to face difficult situations with her. During my adulthood, I continue to find her strength, wisdom, openness, and inquisitiveness guiding me through my personal and professional life. Her life is the example I draw on as I try to live up to the values she embodied.

Val-Kill was not an elegant residence. Originally, it was the factory Grandmère and her friends built in 1927 to employ local men and women before and especially during the hard times of the Depression. Later, it was converted into her home, a place for this world traveler and spokesperson for those without a voice to regenerate herself, a place to be with friends and family in a comfortable, welcoming, but most of all, relaxed setting. My grandmother would not have been able to travel as much or to reach out to people all over the world without those who worked tirelessly and with devotion behind the scenes to maintain Val-Kill and her apartment in New York. The people described in these pages are a few of those who gave of themselves so that Eleanor Roosevelt was cared for during her more private moments. On many occasions I have been asked about my grandmother's most personal moments—who she was when she was not in the spotlight. How she lived at Val-Kill provides at least one example of the foundation of Eleanor Roosevelt's care and appreciation of others. I have described that special world in this memoir because it is in that world that one can observe aspects of her life not typically depicted by her biographers.

CHAPTER 1

Arrival

In 1941, World War II and the Navy brought my parents, John and Anne Roosevelt, from the Boston area to Southern California with their infant son, Haven. My father was stationed in San Diego, where I was born in December 1942. After the war ended, my parents stayed in California, moving first to Berkeley then to Pasadena, where my sister, Sally, was born in December 1946. One day in May 1950, with no explanation, I was told I would get out of school a bit early and that we were moving to New York. Sally and I were too young to even know what to ask—we just did as we were told. Eventually, I realized that we were going to live in Hyde Park, New York, the home of our grandmother, Eleanor Roosevelt.

I had no idea that my grandmother was famous. I had a vague idea that my grandfather had been president, but as a young child, this meant little to me. All I knew about being a Roosevelt was that one of my friends was not allowed to come to my house because of my last name. I later learned that her family referred to my grandfather as "That man!"

Before becoming First Lady, my grandmother focused on bringing women's issues to the forefront. As First Lady, she played a large role in my grandfather's administration, primarily with domestic issues. She traveled throughout the country, seeing for herself how people were living and what problems cities, towns, and rural areas were experiencing, then bringing that information back to her husband in the form of memos describing what she had learned and seen and to which she urged the president to pay attention. It has been reported that Franklin tried to limit the number of memos his wife could send him on a daily basis, to no avail. To some in his administration, she was an annoyance because she was not quiet about what she saw. As her husband's attention turned increasingly to foreign affairs and the war effort, Grandmère continued to remind him about issues at home—poverty, poor health in economically depressed areas, social inequality, failing education, and segregation. During World War II, Grandmère traveled to the war-torn corners of the world to visit soldiers, encouraging and comforting them. After returning from these trips, my grandmother wrote or telephoned the families of wounded soldiers, relaying messages from their loved ones. There was no place my grandmother would not go to learn about the conditions in which people were living and working. I remember a cartoon of my grandmother peering into a mine shaft, two miners at the bottom looking back up the long, dark shaft toward her with quizzical expressions. One miner says to the other, "For gosh sakes, here comes Mrs. Roosevelt."

With the death of her husband, Grandmère retired to Val-Kill, unsure what role she would play in the future. President Truman, however, appointed her in 1945 to the delegation representing the United States at the United Nations General Assembly meeting in London. The only woman, she was elected chair of the Human Rights Commission, whereby she accomplished one of her most significant achievements. By 1948, the Universal Declaration of Human Rights (UDHR) was adopted by the UN General Assembly due largely to Eleanor Roosevelt's commitment, hard work, and political acumen. When the final vote was announced adopting the UDHR resolution, all United Nations delegates stood for an unprecedented standing ovation in honor of her accomplishment. People of color and those living in poverty were aware, during my grandmother's lifetime, of the energy this former First Lady expended in creating more equality in jobs, housing, education, health care, and in the courts. My awareness of who my grand-mother was, however, was just beginning.

It was late May 1950 when we boarded a TWA Jetstream prop plane for the overnight trip from Los Angeles to New York's La Guardia Airport. My brother Haven was nine, I was seven, and my sister Sally was three. We were going to be staying with my grandmother, Eleanor, who was sixty-five and had been widowed for five extremely busy years. In that time, her stature and impact had grown exponentially. I know now that my father was coming home to help with the family farm and to begin his business career in New York City, where he worked for a brokerage firm.

Traveling by airplane during the late 1940s and early '50s was uncommon, which added to the excitement of this adventure. Trips across the country would typically have been by train, which is how we had traveled to attend my grandfather's inauguration for a fourth term as president in 1945. Not long after Franklin died, my mother traveled with Haven and me, together with my bright yellow "potty chair," to visit Eleanor in her New York apartment, which faced Washington Square. I remember waiting on the platform at the Los Angeles train station while the engine of the Super Chief came toward us, growing larger and larger, announcing its powerful elegance. The Super Chief, a shiny, sleek train, eventually came to a steamy, clanking stop in front of us. We boarded the train, and for the next three days I was enthralled by the views of wide-open spaces, towns, and farms as we headed east.

For this cross-country flight, we were dressed according to the custom for travel at the time. My mother wore high heels, a hat, and gloves. My sister and I were dressed in our nice dresses, better than our school dresses but not our velvet Christmas dresses with lace collars. We wanted to wear our favorite patent leather Mary Janes but were told to wear scruffy school shoes. Haven and Daddy wore slacks, ties, and a jacket.

On the plane, Sally and I sat next to each other with Mummy and Daddy facing us. Haven had to sit farther back in the plane, next to a man my mother said was very nice about letting Haven get up and go to the bathroom to put pink calamine lotion on his poison oak rash. Haven, two years older than I, had a bad case of poison oak covering places on his body that we were not allowed to mention. After boarding I immediately forgot about Haven and tried to think about where I was going and what it would be like. We had never been in a plane before, and I knew it would be morning before we got to New York. I was certain Sally would wriggle around, try to take my crayons and chew them, or rip my coloring book and ruin my works of art. Sally was four years younger, and I considered her to be little more than an annoyance.

Shortly before we landed in New York, the stewardess woke us with a breakfast tray. I hated to eat and began pushing the scrambled eggs around my plate when suddenly Sally knocked over her orange juice, drenching my now wrinkled yellow dress. My mother got that look on her face that we understood to mean she'd been around children for too long and we were about to be sent off with our nanny. In the airplane, however, there was no nanny, so Mummy had to get a bunch of napkins and clean up the mess herself while my father looked on in helpless dismay. Just as soon as the orange juice was cleaned up, Sally vomited freshly eaten eggs all over me. Once again, our corner of the plane erupted with my screams, Sally's wails, my mother's exasperated, muffled four-letter words, and my father trying to extricate himself even if it meant squeezing onto the wing of the plane. The stewardess handed me a bunch of damp towels to wipe myself off with, but I could not rid myself of the stink of Sally's half-digested breakfast.

When we landed in New York it was a warm, clear May morning. We were met by Uncle Elliott and his wife, Minnewa, in one car, and by Nate Freeman, a man who worked on my grandmother's farm and was driving a station wagon for the luggage. Nate was a quiet man with a gentle voice whom I would become fond of over the next few months. We three children were sent off with Nate and the luggage. Uncle Elliott, Aunt Minnewa, and my parents planned to drive the last two hours in peace. By this time my parents were harried and glad to rid themselves of the responsibility of one child who might throw up again, one child who reeked of barf, and one who was constantly scratching his crotch. In hindsight, with a parent's perspective, I can't blame them.

The drive to Hyde Park took what seemed to us to be a very long two hours. Sally sat glumly in the back with me. I would have liked to sit in the coveted front passenger seat, next to the window, but Haven always beat me to it, and I knew my wailing protest would bring no sympathy. The drive was not what I had expected: no palm trees, no flowering bushes, and the houses appeared to be built of strange materials. We drove on a four-lane highway through tall buildings with no front yards, and if there was a place to play, it was a concrete parking lot. Eventually, as we left the city heading north on the winding Taconic State Parkway, we saw a few fields with cows, but mostly my view was blocked by large trees. I thought it a strange land.

Having exhausted our constant chorus of, "Are we there yet?," the car was quiet when Nate finally slowed, turned onto a dirt road, and softly announced, "Here we are."

We drove between two stone pillars that were nearly hidden by overgrown vines and low-hanging branches. The dirt road bisected two open fields before passing a small white clapboard cottage where Nate and his wife, Alice, my grandmother's housekeeper, lived. Continuing on we passed a pond, went up over a small hill, past an apple orchard, and then we crossed a rickety wooden bridge that punctuated our arrival with the sound of long boards banging against one another. This was a sound I would grow to love as it was the trumpet that was part of the melodic sounds defining Val-Kill Farm.

Val-Kill Farm was named after the small stream that wandered through the Hudson River Valley property on its way to join larger more important waterways in Dutchess County, New York. Early settlers had combined the Indian name with their own Dutch language, which resulted in the stream being called Val-Kill, meaning "fall creek." The mostly narrow stream widens in front of the Stone Cottage and became what my brother, sisters, and I called "the lake." My mother, however, saw our lake as a mosquito-breeding, snake-filled bog. I now remember it as it was, a lily pond.

The Roosevelt estate was built by my great-grandfather James Roosevelt. Springwood, as it was called, consisted of over one thousand acres stretching from the Hudson River eastward to the top of a hill overlooking the Hudson River Valley. Franklin Roosevelt was born in the Springwood house, which was built high on a bank overlooking the Hudson River. The property surrounding Springwood included greenhouses, stables, a carriage house, and smaller houses for the staff. It was on this stately property that Franklin developed his love of trees, where he spent hours ice-boating, horseback-riding, birding, and working on his stamp collection. What was called the Albany Post Road, now Route 9, separated Springwood from about eight hundred acres of woodlands that continued eastward. Violet Avenue, later named Route 9G, bisected this easterly part of the property. On the west side of Route 9G was a farmhouse surrounded by barns where the animals were kept; on the east side of Route 9G was the property that later was developed into what became Val-Kill, Stone Cottage, and Top Cottage. The last of the homes built on the property, Top Cottage, was built by my grandfather during his presidency as a getaway retreat.

To house the voluminous, twelve-year collection of presidential documents, Franklin designed and built the first presidential library next to the Springwood house. In addition to the documents, both of my grandparents believed that gifts and memorabilia given to them as head of state and First Lady had been given to them as representatives of the American people and should therefore be displayed in the library for them to enjoy. At my grandfather's death, it was decided to transfer the Springwood house, complete with furnishings, books, and photographs, including the presidential library and surrounding acreage, to the government. With Springwood under the care of the National Park Service, the American people could enjoy the house, the beautiful surroundings, and have access to the library's collection of FDR's presidential papers as well as the many personal articles that were part of his life. The remaining land, approximately eight hundred acres, was retained for my grandmother's use.

As we drove on, we saw several buildings clustered together and partially hidden from one another by pine trees and tall hedges. Nate pulled into a drive circling around a crabapple tree that still had some dried-up blooms and buzzing bees. He parked by a stone path leading to a two-story fieldstone house with a high-pitched roof and white trim around its doors and windows, Stone Cottage.

Nate and Alice left Val-Kill several months later, after working for my grandmother for about twelve years. They were always kind to us and seemed to enjoy seeing children running through my grandmother's house. At first, I did not understand and was saddened by their departure, but was finally told that Alice had cancer and was seeking treatment that was not available in Hyde Park. Months later Alice died, and Grandmère acknowledged Alice's death in her long-running, syndicated column, "My Day," where she wrote of the sadness she felt for her friend and housekeeper who had died at such an early age. Nate never returned to the farm.

As I approached the house, drinking in the smell of pine trees, crabapple blossoms, and the dried vomit on my dress, I could barely contain my excitement when I spotted the rectangular swimming pool in front of our house—*Wow!* While looking at the clear blue water and wishing I had my bathing suit, I heard the sound of someone coming through the bushes by the side of the house. I turned and saw my grandmother dressed in a simple cotton house dress taking a shortcut through the peony bushes from her house to greet us. Her broad, toothy smile drew me toward her, and she opened her arms to give me a hug. As my face brushed against her silky, petal-soft cheek, I was far too excited to even worry about the pungent state I was in. If my dress still reeked of the contents of Sally's stomach, Grandmère never showed any sign that she could tell.

In the arrival commotion, I raced off to look for my bedroom in the Stone Cottage, which was right next door to my grandmother's house, Val-Kill Cottage. The Stone Cottage was a house built of fieldstone common to the Hudson River Valley. I entered a small entrance hall. On a corner table was a black telephone with no numbers on it, to the right was a long narrow kitchen, and straight ahead was the dining room. To the left from the entry hall was the living room, a large space with a cathedral ceiling and a huge fireplace built of the same fieldstone used on the outside of the house. During the hot, humid summer days of the Hudson River Valley, the fieldstone kept the downstairs rooms cool. Even in late May the living room was noticeably cooler than outside.

I raced up the stairs that climbed along the wall at the end of the living room opposite the fireplace. Delicate ceramic plates were hung on the wall, staggered to follow the angle of the staircase as I climbed the steps. This seemed strange to me. I remember an American flag in the background of each, announcing the scenes of peaceful life in villages or of raging battles. I later learned that my mother insisted the plates be taken down immediately as they were worth $100 each. She was certain that one of us would knock one off the wall as we raced up and down the stairs. At the landing a small balcony overlooked the living room. Up another two steps and I went through the door into a small dark hallway that opened into a large room with four beds and a couple of bureaus. There were windows on three sides of the room, and where there weren't windows there were empty bookshelves. The four beds, two on the north side of the room and two on the south side, were covered with cotton summer bedspreads, each bedspread in a different color and pattern that stood out against the dark bare floor and the off-white walls. Later I would learn the material had been handwoven by local women. There was one bathroom upstairs and a linen closet. I was dismayed at the thought that I would have to share a room, even a huge one, with Sally and maybe even with Haven. Not to be thrown into distress about this potential disaster, I ran outside to find Rexie.

My Uncle Elliott's wife, Minnewa, had a son from a previous marriage, Rex, who was about my age. I had spent a couple of summers with him in Colorado at his mother's ranch. We had been fearless around the horses and loved putting bridles on any horse we could catch, climbing on without a saddle and riding off into the fields to herd cattle, even though the cattle never seemed to be interested in going in the direction we tried to take them. Rexie was cute, but I definitely did not have a crush on him; in fact, I was always a bit afraid of him because he was a daredevil and I was certain I would be punished if I tried half the things Rexie did. Rexie was at Val-Kill for a couple of weeks, staying in the Top Cottage, the house at the far eastern part of the property. Top Cottage was designed to be wheelchair accessible by my grandfather in 1937–1938 as a place to hide from reporters and leave behind the hectic daily schedule of a president. After FDR's death, my Uncle Elliott had moved into Top Cottage to help my grandmother manage Val-Kill Farm.

I don't remember what Haven and Sally did, but I took off with Rexie on an extra bicycle he had found. Rexie showed me all around the farm, starting with the barns to see the animals. The Jersey dairy cows looked kind and smelled that sweet cow smell unique to dairy cattle. The pigs were twitching their ears to get rid of the flies while they napped, and the chickens never stopped clucking while pecking the ground for any morsel, edible or not. The best part of my tour was swinging from a rope tied to one of the upper beams in the hay loft to the soft pile of hay below. Eventually, we got hungry and returned to the house only to find both our mothers in an agitated state.

It was way past lunch time, and we had missed the Memorial Day ceremony held at the Big House (officially known as Springwood, the FDR Presidential Library and Museum) to honor both my grandfather and those who had died in service to our country. Neither of us knew we were supposed to attend the ceremony, nor did we care; we were glad to have missed it. Who wanted to sit in the hot sun at a ceremony listening to speeches? My mother was furious with me because I was dirty and my pretty yellow dress stained, but she had to leave me as I was because she had not unpacked any of our clothes. I would just have to go through the evening looking like the disheveled but happy child I had become. My grandmother came to my rescue and said, "Anne, dear, Nina is having such a good time with Rexie, it is quite all right that she missed coming to the Big House. It's fine for her to come for dinner as she is—after all, it is only family tonight."

From that moment I had a feeling I would really like the tall, round-shouldered, pewter-haired woman who was called "Grandmère." Grandmère was a name that had always been hard for me to say, so I had gotten used to referring to her as "Gomar," but now I was grown up (seven years old!) and would have to practice saying it the way the French did.

I had seen Grandmère when she and my grandfather occupied the White House, once in New York City, and during her visits to us in California, but I had been too young to remember much about her. I did know that she was my grandmother, and somehow that alone was special.

My maternal grandfather had died before I was born, and I don't remember spending much time with my maternal grandmother. I do remember that my mother told Haven and me that we made too much noise when we were around Gram, as my grandmother was called, which made her nervous. Once we moved to New York, I never saw my maternal grandmother again. Now I was going to get to know my paternal grandmother, and her presence somehow made me lose all fear of my new surroundings.

For the next twelve years, until she died, I spent considerable time with my Grandmère. Being so young, I did not realize how special these years would be. As I grew older, I began to appreciate how both of my grandparents had affected not only me but our country and the world. My parents and my grandmother always talked about what was going on in the present and about the future. Rarely, did anyone talk about past accomplishments. My siblings and I had to learn why our grandparents were famous from other sources. In college I took a course on FDR and the New Deal. I can only imagine what my professor and classmates made of that.

Living next door to my grandmother, it seemed as if we had an extended house. My siblings and I went between Stone Cottage and Val-Kill as if from one room to another.

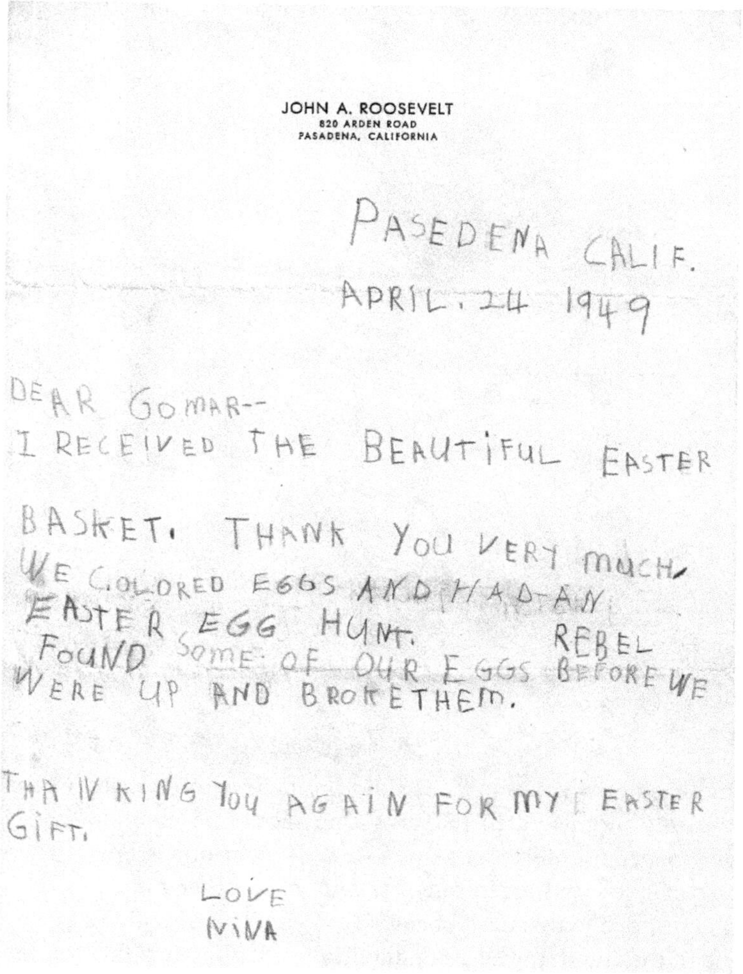

JOHN A. ROOSEVELT
820 ARDEN ROAD
PASADENA, CALIFORNIA

PASEDENA CALIF.
APRIL. 24 1949

DEAR GOMAR--
I RECEIVED THE BEAUTIFUL EASTER BASKET. THANK YOU VERY MUCH.
WE COLORED EGGS AND HAD AN EASTER EGG HUNT. REBEL FOUND SOME OF OUR EGGS BEFORE WE WERE UP AND BROKE THEM.

THANKING YOU AGAIN FOR MY EASTER GIFT.

LOVE
NINA

Figure 1.1. Letter from Nina to Eleanor Roosevelt. *Source*: Personal collection of the author.

It must have been difficult for my mother to suddenly be engulfed by this large Roosevelt family, especially since she had been raised with fewer extended family members. My mother's New England, conservative clan was more involved in finance

Figure 1.2. July 4 in Hyde Park, Eleanor Roosevelt with Nina and Sally.
Source: Photo by G. Brown, FDR Library, public domain.

and business than politics and did not believe in publicity of any sort. My mother often told us, "One should be mentioned in a newspaper no more than three times—when one is born, when one marries, and when one dies, but at no other time."

Added to this clash of cultures, my mother also did not enjoy life in the country, preferring the lively city life. My father, on the other hand, enjoyed the lack of social demands and the quiet of the country. My grandmother was sensitive to my mother's need for privacy and was very careful not to come to Stone Cottage until she knew my mother, a late sleeper, was up and had had a chance to drink her coffee.

My father never seemed to notice what time nor how many people came to the house. While my mother also respected her mother-in-law's privacy, we children ran back and forth between the two houses without notice or invitation. I practiced piano in Grandmère's living room, and on rainy days we watched television or played games in her study. During these times, Grandmère worked at her desk answering all the mail, with her hearing aids turned off so that she was oblivious to the noise we made. Even pillow fights were permitted as long as we did not knock anything over. Joining Grandmère for tea or meals at her house was part of our routine. I also frequently spent the night at my grandmother's. I remember climbing the stairs and around the corner, down a short, narrow hall that led to Grandmère's bedroom; the first door on the left was "my room," actually one of many guestrooms. In the soft glow of a standing lamp, I immediately felt happy, cozy— as if I belonged. To this day I can still hear the gentle swoosh of July's heavy air pushing through the long-needled pine trees that separate my parents' house from Grandmère's. Through the open window, summer air brought the mixture of smells—pine, cedar, garden flowers, and newly mown grass—into the house.

When I stayed overnight with Grandmère, part of her evening ritual was a good-night kiss before I went off to sleep. I well remember one particular night, I was preparing to unfold my long, skinny, pajama-clad body into bed when I heard a soft knock on the door of the bathroom that adjoined Grandmère's bedroom. Grandmère's tall body, slightly stooped by the demands of time, floated into my room. Her long, flowing, white cotton nightgown with a soft, cream-colored robe full of folds transformed her shape into that of a long pillow. Her pewter hair was loose and flowing down her back, caressing her rounded shoulders. Silver hairbrush in hand, Grandmère sat on the edge of my bed slowly brushing her long, thinning, but still vibrant hair. With the rhythm of a slow waltz, she swept her arm gracefully from the top of the right side of her head, easing each tress through the sturdy white bristles. Without a thought I got my own plastic, dime-store, children's hairbrush, sat next to her, and tried to imitate her every move. I started at the top of my short, unruly mop of sandy blonde hair just the way Grandmère did but ran out of hair at the bottom of my earlobe. It did not matter that I would never capture the elegance of my Grandmother's gentle motion, because I knew, as the breeze through the open window encircled our bodies in perfect calm, that this was a moment to treasure.

So many treasured memories of my childhood and adolescence are held in what was originally a furniture factory. In the 1930s, my grandmother's rambling home was the factory building where Val-Kill furniture and crafts were produced. With two friends, Nancy Cook and Marion Dickerman, Grandmère had built Val-Kill Industries, producing simple furniture, handwoven goods, and crafts. The Stone Cottage was built as a place for Nancy Cook and Marion Dickerman to live while they oversaw Val-Kill. In the late 1920s farmers in this predominantly agricultural area were being forced off the land by the rising costs of gas, seed, and fertilizer. Economic disaster, soon to be known as the Great Depression, gripped the country. Working men and women lost their jobs and homes and could no longer feed their families. To answer the crisis in Dutchess County, New York, Grandmère, Nancy, and Marion opened a workshop to make Early American reproduction furniture and other crafts that would offer people a way to supplement their income and create jobs for those out of work. Increasing demands for affordable home furnishings from New York City and the surrounding areas allowed the fledgling company to employ local people, offering an alternative to selling their farms and moving away. Local women also had a place to pursue their interests in crafts and woven goods. In addition to simple maple, pine, walnut, and cherry furniture, pewter vases and wall sconces, and an assortment of woven goods (including bedspreads, dishtowels, and fabrics) were produced and sold by the men and women in what came to be known as Val-Kill Industries. Years later, I still enjoy the simple beauty of Val-Kill furniture, having collected several pieces for my own home. I have always cherished the simplicity of design, craftsmanship, and warmth of the wooden pieces.

Both the Stone Cottage and Grandmère's Val-Kill Cottage were furnished with unsold items from Val-Kill Industries. Typically, the many Val-Kill guestrooms were furnished with a single bed, bureau, slant-front writing desk, and a ladder-back chair all made on site when this building was the Val-Kill furniture factory.

After the closing of Val-Kill Industries in 1938, Nancy Cook and Marion Dickerman, who had contributed so much to Val-Kill and managed the factory, no longer needed to live in the Stone Cottage and moved. My parents initially brought us to stay in the Stone Cottage for the summer; however, we remained there until a few years after my grandmother's death. At the time we came to Val-Kill, my father's brother, Elliott, owned the Top Cottage where he visited when other business obligations permitted. Elliott was managing the farming operations of Val-Kill in 1950. Shortly after we came to Hyde Park, Elliott decided to sell his portion of the Val-Kill Farm property. The Top Cottage was sold to a family named Potter, and much of what had been a Christmas tree farm was also sold at that time. What remained of Elliott's holdings was purchased by my parents. Val-Kill now consisted of my grandmother's Val-Kill Cottage, the Stone Cottage, and a few outbuildings on about two hundred acres of mostly wooded land. It must have been a relief to my grandmother to be able to continue living in the place she had come to love and to have my parents as co-owners help with the maintenance and expenses of the remaining Val-Kill property.

I was pleased to learn that the Val-Kill model was also part of the history of Tucson, Arizona, near where I have lived for many years. My grandmother's bridesmaid and close friend, and the first woman to be elected to Congress from Arizona in 1932, Isabella Greenway, consulted with Grandmère as she developed her own philanthropic furniture shop called the Arizona Hut, to keep people employed after the crash of 1929. Similar to the Val-Kill factory, the Hut employed workers experiencing economic difficulties to make furniture for the newly established Arizona Inn in Tucson. Isabella Greenway's now historic Arizona Inn is filled with furniture that is more reflective of a southwestern design, yet both the Hut and Val-Kill workshops provided necessary employment for families experiencing difficult economic times.

As the Depression eased, agriculture became viable again, and furniture manufacturing shifted to large factories in the South or in Europe. Val-Kill Industries had served its purpose and closed its doors. Despite the factory not turning a profit for its owners, the three women were gratified to have been able to assist the workers and contribute to keeping them off the all-too-common breadlines seen elsewhere. With my grandfather's help, Grandmère turned the factory building into a house she could call her own. Here it was possible for her to escape the formality of the White House and her mother-in-law's Hudson River estate, Springwood.

The Stone Cottage and Val-Kill Farm became home to me and my siblings and the place where we grew up. By September 1952, my sister Joan was a month old, my brother would soon go to the nearby Millbrook School as a boarder, and my sister Sally and I were enrolled in the local elementary school. For the twelve years I had with my Grandmère, I spent considerable time with her, grew close to her, and came to understand why she was so beloved throughout the world.

We experienced the wonders of traveling to exotic places, welcomed world leaders and luminaries, endured family tragedies, and shared the love of our Hudson River Valley home, Val-Kill Farm, together.

CHAPTER 2

Extended Family

The Curnans and the Entrups

As soon as I came to Val-Kill, I learned that the Roosevelts had relied on the Curnan family for three generations and that the Curnans had become an extended part of our family. Charlie Curnan began by working for Sara Delano Roosevelt in the gardens at Springwood. Only his Army service interrupted his connection with our family. My father and grandmother returned this loyalty and employed several of the Curnan family members to help them manage the household as well as the extensive grounds that made up Val-Kill Farm. My father considered Charlie a brother. Charlie was the farm's superintendent, and as children we knew his word was to be obeyed. That said, Charlie was a kind, hard worker and was always patient with us and willing to take the time to show us how to do various things around the farm. No one could ever make onion, green pepper, and tomato sauce like Charlie's. Charlie drove me to school, saving me the long walk when the weather was cold and rainy, and it was Charlie whom we called with any emergency. As I grew older, it was Charlie's advice that replayed in my head as I negotiated adolescence. Charlie warned me to watch how others treated animals. To Charlie, if animals showed an instant dislike of a person or the person did not treat animals with respect, that was a person to avoid.

Charlie's steadfast loyalty to our family and the warmth of his smile made him someone I looked up to. I continue to think of him fondly. Charlie's brothers, Pat and "Tubby" (Archibald), as well as Charlie's wife, Millie, all took care of our family in various capacities as long as we lived at Val-Kill.

With his Army service behind him, Charlie worked most of his life for our family and was responsible for just about everything. Maintaining the several houses, lawns, gardens, agricultural crops, outbuildings, and the long dirt driveway was a full-time job. We were all expected to pitch in and help.

Each summer my grandmother's niece, Eleanor Roosevelt Elliott (Hall Roosevelt's daughter), came to Val-Kill for a month or more with her four children—Stewart, Ted, Lauren, and Eleanor Elliott. In addition to Charlie's responsibilities for maintaining the estate, he was essentially a camp counselor keeping the four of us, the four Elliotts, and my cousin John Boettiger too busy to

Figure 2.1. Silver platter presented to Charlie Curnan to honor years of service. *Source*: Personal collection of the author.

Figure 2.2. Charlie Curnan with John, Eleanor Roosevelt, and Anne.
Source: Personal collection of the author.

get in trouble. He ran a tight ship and made sure we were useful. He took the time to teach us how to do the tasks he assigned to contribute to this wonderful place that we were so fortunate to be a part of. He even taught us how to work as a team, which made the chores more efficient.

We were responsible for stacking fireplace wood in the cellars of both Val-Kill Cottage and Stone Cottage. We took our ancient Farmall tractor with a flatbed trailer into the woods where Charlie had small piles of chopped wood ready to be picked up and brought to the cellars. We established a line to pass the wood from one to another, ultimately up to the flatbed. Putting the wood in the cellars was more difficult because of the stairs that led down into them, and one of the stronger of us would be in charge of this part of the task. The younger ones did not mind since the cellars were dark and dusty and intimidating.

Figure 2.3. "Wood for the Winter by Eleanor Roosevelt II." *Source*: Elliott/ Roosevelt family personal collection.

By July the hay was ready to be mowed, baled, and brought to our barn. We grew hay in the fields of Val-Kill but often needed more than we produced and had to purchase it from local farmers. I remember once we even went to Springwood, now managed by the National Park Service, to pick up bales of hay for our barn. At Val-Kill, as soon as the hay had been baled, we were responsible for picking it up and bringing the hay to our barn before it could be rained on. There was no easy way to get the heavy bales from the flatbed up to the loft. Instead of an electric elevator or conveyor belt to make this task a great deal easier, we had to manually get the hay to the opening and then stack it, starting in the back of the barn. None of us, even Haven, were strong enough to throw the hay into place. We again passed each bale from one to the other while at least two of us stood on the rungs of a long ladder, wrestling the bales just a bit higher to the next person in line. A couple of us were responsible for being close to the roof where the ladder touched the hay-mow door to drag each bale to the back, stacking it neatly in rows at least four bales high. This was a particularly hot job in the humidity of the Hudson River Valley!

Regardless of the season, our other constant job was repairing the long dirt driveway from Route 9G to my grandmother's house. The potholes in that road seemed to multiply faster than rabbits. Again, we took the tractor and flatbed to our gravel pit to load gravel and then distribute it into potholes, tamping the gravel down as we hoped it would stay longer than the next rain. It rarely did.

Looking back, I realize that being older and male was a distinct advantage. My brother, Haven, was the eldest and also the strongest, which allowed him to appoint himself our leader. None of us dared challenge Haven's authority, so when he could, he always chose the easiest jobs for himself. With the exception of the youngest, each of us knew how to drive the tractor, but somehow Haven always took that particular job, which left all the heavy lifting to the rest of us. All of us were adept at trying to get one of the others to do the less desirable tasks, such as stacking wood in the dusty, dark cellars by claiming an allergy or just by being so slow the others would realize we'd never finish in time to go for a swim. Even the youngest members of our team contributed in any way they were able, which sometimes meant just playing in the dirt while the rest of us sweated and groaned under the weight of the hay bales or had aching arms from shoveling gravel for the road.

During the first summers at Val-Kill, we also worked in the vegetable garden, which I remember mostly had tomato plants and rows of strawberries. The tomatoes needed to be canned during the hottest, most humid days of the summer. It always seemed rather like torture to stand in the kitchen with the ripe tomatoes being squished into jars and then put into big canning steamers filled with water, heated on the stove, and left to boil for what felt like hours. Everything was swathed in water. Steam rising from the boiling jars clung to the walls and ceiling, dripping down to the floor. My mother seemed to be wilting as sweat covered her entire body. Both my grandmother's kitchen and ours went through this melting activity until my grandmother discovered the farmers market and their constant supply of fresh vegetables. It was a great relief when canning tomatoes was abandoned. We concentrated on fresh corn, which was a much easier job. My mother was a corn snob and believed Silver Queen was the best variety of corn. Charlie planted a section of our field with this corn for her, which we then had to pick and put in the freezer, fortunately avoiding the canning process altogether. Grandmère also enjoyed the corn, so we prepared about two hundred ears of corn for each house. In the early fall, when the apples in the orchard were ripe, we rushed to pick them before the birds were able to ruin their pristine look.

One of the highlights of the summer for my grandmother was the arrival of the boys from the Wiltwyck School for their annual picnic at Val-Kill. The Wiltwyck School, in Esopus, New York, across the Hudson River from Hyde Park, was a home for young boys who had been adjudicated as juvenile delinquents, as well as some who were considered to be at high risk for behavioral problems. Wiltwyck focused on developing their students into productive members of society. Moral and spiritual growth, character development, education, and good citizenship were the founding principles on which the school operated. My grandmother had been committed, since the late 1930s, to helping Wiltwyck develop as a model for acknowledging that children suffering from poverty and abusive, dangerous home environments, when given the chance, could turn their fear, anger, traumas, and abandonment into productive behaviors without being incarcerated.

Grandmère often took people who were role models to visit the school. My cousin, Ellie Seagraves, remembers going with our grandmother on a visit with Marian Anderson, who sang folk songs and spirituals for the boys. Paul Robeson also entertained the boys as a guest of Grandmère's. Ellie remembers the boys being thrilled "with his deep voice full of passion and shadings, and a consummate role model for the youngsters." Not only did the boys enjoy meeting people from various fields of achievement, but this was also a way to introduce people of financial means to the needs of Wiltwyck. Harry Belafonte gave many hours to nurture the boys at the school and helped them to form a steel drum band and record their songs. Grandmère, in her "My Day" column, commented on how thankful she was to Mr. Belafonte for giving these boys such an experience.

"He has given the boys at Wiltwyck School a chance to learn to make and to use steel drums, and they have made some fine recordings and developed considerable talent, even appearing on a show in Carnegie Hall," she wrote. "This is a great outlet for boys like this who need sometimes to express themselves with violence and who can do it safely on the drums!" I still have my copy of the Wiltwyck Steel Drum recording that Grandmère gave me for Christmas.

As soon as Grandmère moved into Val-Kill, she would invite all the boys from the school to come for daylong picnics, establishing a much-loved summer ritual. As each boy got off the

Figure 2.4. Eleanor Roosevelt serving hot dogs at Wiltwyck picnic. *Source*: Elliott/Roosevelt family personal collection.

bus, Grandmère greeted them with a warm smile that was only matched by the excitement in the boys' steps as they ran around playing games on the grass. The picnic was a time for everyone at Val-Kill—staff, family, and guests—to entertain these eager youngsters. We served hot dogs, potato salad, baked beans, and Neapolitan ice cream for dessert. Grandmère, the head server, was joined by the Elliott children, my siblings and me, all of the Val-Kill staff, and whatever other cousins might have been there at the time.

After lunch, Grandmère sat on a large log with the boys settled around her while she read stories from Kipling's *Just So Stories*. There was no doubt to anyone who was there and saw the smile and joy in her eyes that this was a special day for my grandmother.

Figure 2.5. Eleanor Roosevelt reading to boys from Wiltwyck. *Source*: Elliott/Roosevelt family personal collection.

The genuine good will and kindness shown by Grandmère made it clear that she truly cared about these young boys. Tired, but happy, at the end of the day the boys gathered around my grandmother to thank her. Some of the younger ones even threw their arms around her to engulf her in a joyous hug. From the open windows of the bus, the boys waved and shouted, "See you next year, Mrs. Roosevelt!"

℃

Late in the summer of 1952, when Haven was eleven and I was nine, we were both taken seriously ill. Haven was stricken first, and when I woke up several days later with aching legs and an inability to stand without holding on to the bed frame, I knew I had whatever he'd contracted. Mother had just given birth to my youngest sister, Joan, and in order to protect her newborn from catching the disease, Haven and I were sent to my grandmother's house, where we were more isolated. An official diagnosis was not discussed in front of either of us, but we overheard the word *polio* and saw downcast eyes. We were aware that our grandfather had contracted polio, but somehow, in our minds, that was a long time ago. Haven, with a milder case, was able to move around more freely and was soon able to go back to his room in the Stone Cottage. I was confined to bed. Grandmère often came into my room with a smile and acted as if I had the flu and would be out of bed soon. The magnitude of my parents' and grandmother's concern was apparent when a polio specialist, and a vice president of the American Medical Association, arrived at Val-Kill and suggested that a rehabilitation center would be appropriate as I probably would never walk without difficulty.

We were a family that believed in the stiff upper lip and suppressed anxiety. Surely, having watched his father struggle with polio, my father must have been afraid for Haven and me. However, he never showed concern in front of us. Daddy was a child of five when his father came down with polio, and my grandfather never walked without aid again. FDR's polio denied my father the robust engagement that his elder brothers had enjoyed with my grandfather as they grew up. In order to try to recover the use of his legs, FDR spent months in Florida and Warm Springs, Georgia, trying any rehabilitation program that may have been suggested to him. Furthermore, when my grandfather decided to reengage with his political career, his campaigns demanded time and travel away from home. From the age of five on, I believe my father felt the loss of his father to both polio and politics. When his children came down with the same disease, it may have been that my father was faced with reliving those lonely years. My father did not come into my room unless my grandmother, mother, or a doctor was also in the room.

Fortunately, my grandmother's close friend, Dr. David Gurewitsch, had medical training that included rehabilitation techniques not typically used in the United States. David did not agree with the first doctor's assessment that I would not be able to walk without braces. David offered to work with me to regain strength in my legs.

David Gurewitsch was born in Switzerland shortly after his parents emigrated there from Russia. While receiving medical training in Germany, David met Trude Lash, who later introduced him to her friend, Eleanor Roosevelt. David and my grandmother shared personal experiences and values and established a close friendship that lasted until my grandmother died. Both were shy, both had their own insecurities, and both were intellectually curious and had the capacity for deep empathy for others. David was a caring, compassionate physician, and my grandmother gave her passionate energy to all who were less fortunate the world over.

By the time I became his patient, Dr. Gurewitsch was affiliated with Columbia-Presbyterian Hospital in rehabilitation and had become a polio specialist. In the beginning of my recovery, David came to see me daily to oversee my exercises and hot baths and evaluate my progress. As unusual as it may sound, David taught me how to fall—to relax before I went to the floor. David was concerned that if I ever fell and injured one of my legs, regaining muscle strength would be more difficult. He was always kind and especially gentle. I came to have great affection for David, whose demeanor made you feel as if he knew you, that he understood things you could not even articulate. To a nine-year-old, this was extraordinary, and it helped me do everything he suggested, even though I hated the exercises he prescribed. It never occurred to me that David's instructions wouldn't lead to a full recovery, as there was no discussion in front of me that would lead me to believe that there was anything seriously wrong with me. Grandmère surely worried, but she did not share her concern with me. Instead, she took action. It was Grandmère who asked her friend to accept me as a patient, and she helped my parents, who were skeptical of everything outside of traditional therapies, to accept Dr. Gurewitsch's somewhat new techniques for rehabilitation in my case.

Part of my recovery regimen was to take hot baths twice a day. At this time my grandmother had a butler named William White.

Figure 2.6. William White, Eleanor Roosevelt's butler. *Source*: Elliott/ Roosevelt family personal collection.

William was responsible for carrying me from my bed and gently sliding me into the hot water, then retrieving me from the bath and putting me back in bed. I could not stand even briefly and had to rely on others caring for me in the beginning. I was shy and did not want to be naked in front of anyone but William. He respectfully covered my skinny, undeveloped, naked body with towels to save me embarrassment, and I never wanted anyone

Figure 2.7. Raising money for the March of Dimes, Nina and Haven with Eleanor Roosevelt, 1953. *Source*: *New York Herald Tribune*, public domain.

to put me in or take me out of the bathtub except William. Hot baths continued for a few months. Gradually an exercise routine contributed to my being able to go back to school before Christmas. While I never regained complete strength on my left side, David Gurewitsch's instructions for balance and continued exercise enabled me to recover with few residual effects.

Besides being a kind and considerate man, William was noted for his incredible ability to play ping-pong. (I believe he had won various tournaments during his service in the U.S. Army.) William taught my brother and my cousin, John Boettiger, how to play ping-pong, and they became formidable players. We were all sad when William left Val-Kill to pursue other career opportunities.

Beginning with Memorial Day and throughout the summer and fall, Val-Kill was a busy place.

It was important to have help, especially in the kitchen, for all the meals that needed to be served. Early one spring my grandmother was notified, just prior to a planned gathering for

Figure 2.8. Eleanor Roosevelt ties a bow in Sally's hair. *Source*: Elliott/Roosevelt family personal collection.

Figure 2.9. Elliott and Roosevelt families at Val-Kill picnic. *Source*: Elliott/ Roosevelt family personal collection.

the weekend at Val-Kill, that her cook had quit. It was a Thursday, and Grandmère was in New York City, unable to interview a new cook. On Friday Grandmère spent a busy day in her office at the United Nations, not leaving until late in the afternoon to drive the two hours to Val-Kill. As Grandmère walked down the long steps in front of the UN, a short, thin, gray-haired woman, her face drawn in pain, with clear blue, expressive eyes, and walking with a distinct limp, approached her. Irene's limp might have been the first thing people noticed, but the blue eyes told Grandmère a story of unfathomable pain and fear. Irene moved as fast as she could along the uneven steps, waving her arms to balance her body, and called out to my grandmother.

"Oh, Mrs. Roosevelt, Mrs. Roosevelt!" the woman cried in heavily German-accented English. "Do you know where I can find a job?"

My grandmother looked at the woman, immediately recognizing a concentration camp survivor by the tattooed number on her arm, which Irene had tried to hide with a sleeve that was too short. Then Grandmère glanced at her watch and said, "Can you be ready in half an hour? Where will I find you?"

When the interview was over, Irene was hired on the spot. A very excited Irene gave Grandmère the address of a shelter for refugees, and within the hour Grandmère had picked up her new cook and they were on their way to Val-Kill. Grandmère never asked Irene if she could cook, and as we learned later, she wasn't much of a cook. Ultimately, that did not matter as there were many other jobs that needed to be done in Grandmère's household for which Irene was suited.

I remember Irene as someone who broke my young heart. Her strained face, the fear permanently expressed in her eyes, haunts me nearly seventy years later. Irene remained excitable and in chronic pain as a result of her treatment in the concentration camp, where, beside starvation and disease, her leg was broken and never properly healed. Irene later said that she had been the victim of medical experiments while in the concentration camp. Irene proved a kind, loyal employee for my grandmother and a woman we all loved. Irene was assured by the family and the Gurewitsches that she would be cared for until her death, which came not long after Grandmère's death.

Memorial Day, a special day for our family, included a wreath-laying ceremony and speeches at the FDR gravesite and presidential library, followed by a luncheon in honor of national and local dignitaries hosted by my grandmother at Val-Kill, as well as a tea later in the afternoon for the Roosevelt Home Club and any others interested in meeting the keynote speaker. One of my grandmother's favorite Memorial Day speeches was in 1957, the year Sputnik's launch had Americans worried about the power of the Soviet Union. Violence was erupting in the South, requiring federal troops to enforce school integration in Little Rock, Arkansas. Edward G. Robinson, the actor, was the keynote speaker that year, and my grandmother commented in her "My Day" column, "Edward G. Robinson spoke of Franklin D. Roosevelt's interest in people. I think Mr. Robinson touched the hearts of his audience more than anyone who has ever spoken there. His speech was poetic and moving."

Shortly after Irene had been hired as the cook, Charlie knew that our yearly Memorial Day luncheon and tea would be more than Irene could comfortably handle. Charlie needed to find extra help for this especially busy time. Marge and Les Entrup, a couple Charlie had known for years, had recently sold their Hyde Park restaurant. Charlie tried to convince the Entrups to come work at Val-Kill. Charlie's pleas were rebuffed, especially by Marge who did not think Eleanor Roosevelt would want Republicans working for her, even in an emergency. Les, however, did agree to Charlie's request to help out but only for the Memorial Day weekend. Later, Charlie persisted, knowing that Grandmère needed help in the kitchen and around the house, and he was convinced that the Entrups had the experience of handling large crowds and would be just the right fit for our unconventional life at Val-Kill.

Grandmère needed a cook who was used to managing large numbers of people as well as individual dietary needs. My grandmother was not an accomplished cook herself, nor did she really seem to care what the food tasted like as long as there was enough for everyone and the conversation at the table was engaging and interesting. Grandmère's lack of interest in how food tasted during the White House years has been noted by her biographers. The rest of us, however, were eager for the Entrups to come to work. My cousin, John Boettiger, later said, "Thank God for Marge." He went on to explain that if we had relied on our grandmother's cooking, we would eat nothing but scrambled eggs. Additionally, it was important for whoever was helping in the kitchen to be able to go to the grocery at a moment's notice, serve in the dining room, and help with the mountain of dishes. Charlie decided to continue talking with Marge and Les to see if they could be convinced to at least try working for my grandmother. At first Marge, assuming that my grandmother would want gourmet food, continued to be adamant that she would not want to work at Val-Kill. Over time, with Charlie's gentle coaxing, Marge finally said that as long as she would not be expected to cook "pheasant under glass," she would agree to cook "down-to-earth, good food." At last, the food at Val-Kill was really good, and an enduring bond of friendship and respect between my grandmother and the Entrups, in spite of their political allegiances, began.

Marge and Les, with their daughter, Janet, moved into the apartment attached to the main part of Val-Kill.

The Entrups' elder daughter, Barbara, had married Pat Curnan, Charlie's youngest brother. Charlie had hired Pat to work for the family, helping to care for the farm animals that came and went, depending on my father's whims of being a responsible land owner. Whatever misgivings Marge may have had soon evaporated as she and my grandmother developed a mutual respect and a

Figure 2.10. Marge, Les, and Janet Entrup. *Source*: Entrup family personal collection.

working relationship that became a true friendship. Grandmère enjoyed being a part of the meal planning but, as her respect for Marge's capabilities increased, she began turning much of the day-to-day operation of her home over to Marge, although they did still discuss the menu plans. It was Marge who had the final say about what would work and what would not.

Marge knew what certain Val-Kill guests liked and did not like and always tried to accommodate them.

Marge and my grandmother's warm relationship went beyond day-to-day meal planning. Grandmère sought Marge's advice on personal matters as well. In spite of her general warmth and inclusiveness, my grandmother was cautious, especially in regard to her family, and did not embrace actions she believed could be fraught with unseen consequences, opting for a slow, methodical approach.

Uncle Elliott, who had four children from previous marriages, married a woman with four children from her own previous

Figure 2.11. Val-Kill staff: Irene, Becky, Marge, and Les. *Source*: FDR Library, public domain.

Figure 2.12. Eleanor Roosevelt and Marge supervise lunch by the pond.
Source: Elliott/Roosevelt family personal collection.

marriage. My uncle and his wife decided that he should legally adopt her children and change their name to Roosevelt. Grandmère was concerned because the children's biological father was living, and the children were just beginning to get used to a new family situation. My grandmother felt that this decision should be made with caution, fearing the children involved might be confused. Grandmère believed in Marge's compassion and her ability to realize the complications such a decision could bring with it. It is not known what advice Marge may have given, but I do remember my grandmother telling my mother that she was concerned but felt she should not intervene. Uncle Elliott's family was extended to include four more children, and I remember wondering when we would meet these new cousins and how they would adapt to the large Roosevelt family and changing their last name to one they would need to get used to. As it turned out, I only met two of my new cousins but not until many years after my grandmother's death.

Figure 2.13. Eleanor Roosevelt, Marge, Les, Les's sister (standing). *Source*: Entrup family personal collection.

The entire extended Entrup family came to love my grandmother. Relatives of Marge and Les often came to Val-Kill to enjoy swimming in the summer or skating on the pond in the winter.

It was a relationship built on mutual respect, kindness, openness, and appreciation for the strengths and weakness of each. The Entrups worked as a family. Daughters Barbara and Janet pitched in whenever extra help was needed and were always happy to do so. Janet and I were the same age and attended the same school. We have remained in touch for more than fifty years. Janet said, "My teenage years, growing up in the 1950s and early '60s, most of all I remember Val-Kill. There are so many wonderful memories of those days, even small events that were special just because Mrs. Roosevelt and her family and a vast number of friends were involved."

Grandmère, always sensitive to others, saw in Janet a quiet shyness built on a strong sense of responsibility and kindness.

Janet spent many hours in the kitchen, which was too small to accommodate a dishwasher, helping her parents wash dishes and whatever other tasks were necessary. Janet was certain that the family employer would not have noticed her, but she was mistaken.

Grandmère had been alerted that the family who would be living in Hyde Park for the summer to manage the Hyde Park Playhouse needed someone to look after their young children, including an infant. Janet remembers my grandmother coming to her and asking if she would be willing to babysit for this family. Janet knew this would be a huge job and was surprised that Mrs. R. (as she called my grandmother) had even noticed her. The Playhouse staff worked from morning until late in the evening with little time for meals or breaks. After giving the idea some thought, Janet did decide to take on this responsibility. What Janet learned was the gift Eleanor Roosevelt had given her by believing in and having confidence in her as a young girl who would be able to take on this responsibility.

Later, as Janet was preparing to graduate from high school, her guidance counselor, Miss Wood, asked what college she planned to attend after graduation. Janet, knowing that her family had unexpected medical expenses and did not have the funds for her to continue her education, told Miss Wood that she planned to get some sort of job and would continue her education at a later time. Assuming the subject to be closed, Marge, Les, and Janet were shocked when, a few days later, Maureen Corr, my grandmother's longtime secretary and friend, came to them and told them that my grandmother wanted to talk to them in her study. Marge and Les were mystified as to why they were all being asked to come to see Grandmère in her study. Janet feared she had done something wrong. She recalls that my grandmother told Marge and Les that the guidance counselor had told her that Janet was postponing her dream of going to nursing school. To my grandmother this was unacceptable, so she offered to pay the necessary fees so that Janet could continue her education in the fall. Les was, of course, mortified and objected, saying that he would figure something out and Janet could go in a year or so.

My grandmother then said, "I do this for people I don't know! What makes you think I would not want to do this for Janet?" Needless to say, my grandmother prevailed and Janet went on to nursing school in Burlington, Vermont.

While in Burlington, at the end of one semester, Janet came down with pneumonia. She had to be hospitalized and would not be well enough to make the trip home for the holiday break. My grandmother called one day to check on how Janet was feeling and asked to speak with her.

The nurse answering the phone asked, "Who is calling?"

"This is Eleanor Roosevelt," my grandmother answered.

The nurse, who enjoyed playing practical jokes on the nursing students, assumed that the students had finally found a way to reciprocate and play a joke on her. So, she said, "If you're Eleanor Roosevelt, then I'm Harry S. Truman." And *click*, she hung up.

Eventually, Grandmère did talk with Janet, who remembers that "Mrs. R. asked how I was feeling, was I comfortable, and did I have everything I needed. She also wanted to know if she should send a specialist from the city to make sure I was recovering."

Janet, always the most thoughtful person, found a gift that became one of my grandmother's favorites. Weather permitting, we often ate meals on my grandmother's screened-in porch, which was quite a distance from the kitchen. Marge would have the first course at the table, but when that was finished and the dishes needed to be cleared before the next course, my grandmother would ring a small crystal bell. The sound barely traveled through the house, and Marge, unable to hear the bell, was left not knowing it was time for the table to be cleared and the next course served. Janet, while at a craft fair, saw a brass gong and thought it would be perfect, as its crash would be loud enough to summon her mother. Janet bought the gong for my grandmother, and it was used from then on. This gong, like the boards on the wooden bridge, was one of the sounds, like a signature, that was unique to our lives at Val-Kill.

Every spring, waiting for us by the edge of "the lake" were two small row boats ready to be scraped, caulked, and repainted.

Figure 2.14. Eleanor Roosevelt, Sally, Nina with Fala on leash, Tamas to the left. *Source*: *Look*, 1951.

The largest one was tied to a crooked, weathered, wooden dock, and the other flat-bottomed boat was pulled up on the grass with only its stern touching the water.

We used the boats—creatively named "big boat" and "little boat"—to conduct serious water fights and to catch small sunfish with whatever we could put together as a fishing pole. By the end of the summer, the pond had filled with so many lily pads and so much thick algae that our water fights consisted of throwing slimy green muck.

The lily pads that covered the west end of the pond made thick, platter-sized, green platforms that floated on top of the water. Their green leaves overlapping one another suggested a comfortable bed—I imagined they would hold me afloat while the water gently rocked me. The lilies did provide sturdy perches for the hundreds of bullfrogs that formed what had to be the loudest bass choir in New York. During the summer months, every night around dusk a deep, a guttural, solo croak would pierce the silence. After a pause, a loud chorus of long, equally throaty croaks would begin, shattering any notions of a quiet country evening. The frogs were singing! In some ways it sounded like the on-and-off honking of a traffic jam. For those not accustomed to this seemingly endless cacophony, sleep was nearly impossible. The slightest disturbance in the otherwise peaceful, rhythmical night caused the frogs to jump back into the pond with short *ker-plunks* as they disappeared underwater. Suddenly, all was silent. Then, as if an imaginary conductor raised their baton, and without preamble, the Val-Kill chorus would begin again.

To complement the tenor and bass notes of the Val-Kill Frog Orchestra, cicadas sang the soprano sections, while fireflies blinked their lights on and off, not necessarily in sync with either the cicadas or the more rhythmical frogs. These sparkles of light made it look as if little stars were dangling and playing tag over the lawn and pond. The fireflies, with help from the moon, allowed the white and yellow blooms of the lilies to glow in the dark. If the mosquitoes had not played their own annoying tunes on these nights, we would have gladly slept outside on the lawn beside the pond. Because she loved to be engulfed by the sound of the frog chorus, a signal of peace and tranquility, Grandmère slept on her screened-in sleeping porch facing the pond during the summers.

By morning all was quiet until the birds awoke and the rising sun signaled the lilies that it was time to close and sleep. These early morning sounds were my cue to get up and try to leave Stone Cottage as quietly as possible so as not to awaken my parents and siblings, who were definitely not morning people. Grandmère rose early to take her dogs, Fala (FDR's famed black Scottie) and Tamas, a younger black Scottie, for walks through the woods. (After Fala died, Duffy joined the Scottie clan.) Each morning I waited impatiently in my bedroom for the sound of the screen door at Val-Kill Cottage to bang shut and for Grand-mère's high-pitched voice to call out, "Here, Fala! Here, Fala! Here, Tamas! Here, Tamas!" These sounds were my signal to run down the stairs and join the morning walk. Grandmère knew I would be joining her, and as soon as she saw me, she smiled, said, "Good morning, Nina," and picked up her normal pace. We headed into the woods silently at first, listening for the birds and looking for chameleons or any little toads or lizards that scurried out of our way. Whenever we found a chameleon, Grandmère would help me move it so that we could watch it change color to match the colors of its new surroundings. Grandmère taught me the names of some of the wildflowers we saw, though I forgot most of them. Queen Anne's lace, with its dainty little white buds reaching away from a tiny black velvet dot in the center, was my favorite. Though it really did resemble lace, I never understood why it was called "Queen Anne's" lace. During the first part of our walk, Fala and Tamas raced ahead, but their advanced age soon caught up with them and they straggled along behind us. Grandmère's long stride kept us moving at a quick pace, and my shorter child's legs had a hard time keeping up with her. When the deer flies and mosquitoes began to bite us, we turned around and headed back for breakfast.

The breakfast table was always laid with an assortment of jams, jellies, Val-Kill honey, and bread. The table itself was carefully set with silver pots containing hot coffee, tea, and hot water. Grandmère poured a little bit of tea into her cup, then filled it to the top with water. It looked to me as if she really wanted colored hot water with a bit of milk with breakfast. Grandmère would pour our juice, coffee, or tea and ask if anyone would like oatmeal. I don't think she ever realized that eating porridge was an outdated custom. I never saw anyone eat hot oatmeal during our summer breakfasts. Yet the familiar, covered, oval dish full of oatmeal was a permanent fixture on Grandmère's breakfast table.

During the warmer months, by nine in the morning most guests had risen and gathered around one of the two long tables on the screened-in porch for a hearty breakfast. Summer mornings were not complete without the sound of the piercing screech as the wooden porch chairs were pulled back and forth across the smooth cement floor of the porch—a sound more startling than any alarm clock! Several intervals of screeching faded into initially muted talk as all the guests settled around the table, accented by the gong Janet had given my grandmother. By the time the coffee took hold, the conversation grew louder and could be heard clearly in our house next door. Uninitiated guests admitted that the loud nightly frog chorus had shattered their notion of a quiet night's sleep in the country. Occasionally, others complained about the level of noise that the "young people" made while swimming late at night.

Fearful that our sometimes raucously bad language could be heard, we were grateful that Grandmère removed her hearing aids at night.

Marge was as happy cooking for thirty-five people as she was for five. The guests could request whatever kind of eggs or special breakfast food they liked, and Marge would deliver perfect dishes every time. Unlike some of my grandmother's previous cooks, who had been hired out of compassion rather than for any culinary skill, Marge was a good cook. Grandmère never had to worry about whether the meals would be on time.

Figure 2.15. Val-Kill summer. Back row: Lauren, Forbes Morgan, Haven, John Boettiger, Stewart, Ted; front row: guest, Sally, Barbara Morgan, Nina with Joan, Eleanor. *Source:* personal collection of the author.

After breakfast, before it got too hot, Grandmère, accompanied by her two Scotties, often went to attend to her flower garden. Grandmère enjoyed flowers and took pleasure arranging flowers for every room in her house. If Grandmère had a favorite flower, I guess it would be roses, as she grew beautiful rosebushes in her garden, along with gladiolas and zinnias. One of my favorite images is of Grandmère, wearing a brown and deep gold African wraparound skirt, a white sleeveless blouse, and a wide-brimmed straw hat that cast a gentle screen to protect her face from the sun, surrounded by sweet smelling, multicolored rosebushes. Her tall figure would bend over, shaped almost like an upside-down U, to examine the roses ready for cutting. Her clippers would be in one hand, a flat basket with gently sloping sides resting just above the wrist of her other hand, and, as was Grandmère's habit when concentrating, she would chew her tongue.

Guests at Val-Kill were always greeted with a small fresh flower arrangement in their bedrooms. Grandmère had a collection of small flower vases that she filled with three or four flowers, some wild and some from her garden, that she personally replaced when they wilted. I sometimes watched her arrange the flowers and would trail behind her, carrying as many little vases as I could upstairs to the guest bedrooms. Grandmère was often preoccupied at these times, yet her face looked calm and serene, her head bobbing gently up and down, assessing each flower and the little arrangements she was creating.

I liked spending time with Grandmère in her garden and, with her encouragement, I even tried to plant a small vegetable garden of my own. I planted rows of lettuce, carrots, and scallions that produced little. Grandmère suggested I plant summer squash, assuming it would be easier for me to grow. Knowing that I would have to eat whatever I managed to grow to maturity, I chose not to grow things I didn't like. After working on her roses, Grandmère would stroll over to my very crooked rows of fledgling lettuce and advise me how to fertilize and water the plants. Unless Grandmère was in the garden with me, I forgot to water the few survivors and eventually they began to wilt as the days grew hotter and hotter. As an adult I have continued to grow a few flowers and vegetables, which has allowed me to understand the peace my grandmother must have felt while quietly admiring the miracle of each plant as it grew to maturity. I am proud to say my planting and watering technique has improved with age.

CHAPTER 3

Forays in Dutchess County

Grandmère's morning routine included working at her desk in what we called "Tommy's Living Room," where she wrote her five-hundred-word "My Day" column. She never missed a deadline and produced over seven thousand articles, which were distributed to hundreds of newspapers across the country. She also answered the stacks of letters she received from people in every corner of the world. Her work space was called Tommy's Living Room after Malvina Thompson—known as "Tommy"—who had been my grandmother's assistant for years and was a second mother to my father. The renovation of Val-Kill Cottage from furniture factory to home included an apartment for Tommy within the house. By the time I came to Val-Kill, Tommy was partially retired and mostly helped Grandmère when she was in Hyde Park. In New York my grandmother's assistant was Maureen Corr, who continued to work in both New York and at Val-Kill after Tommy died in 1953. Tommy and Maureen were beloved friends of my grandmother, with whom they worked and traveled.

Before starting to work at her desk, Grandmère met with Marge Entrup to plan meals for the guests staying at Val-Kill as well as for those invited for tea, luncheon, or dinner. Grandmère, sensitive to the cultural eating habits of her visitors, relied on Marge's expertise to offer food that could be enjoyed by all. When I was about twelve, the two of them were discussing menus for the weekend guests, and I overheard Grandmère tell Marge, "As we have thirty-six for dinner tonight and nearly as many for meals tomorrow, I'll just go across the river to the vegetable stand for the vegetables."

Marge responded, "In that case, you could get more carrots, string beans, and tomatoes. I have my hands full with the meals for this weekend. Do you think they would have corn this early in the season?"

"I wouldn't think so, but I'll look."

Grandmère's favorite fruit and vegetable market was near Kingston on the west bank of the Hudson River. On this particular July trip to buy vegetables, I accompanied Grandmère to the market, where she saw some delicious-looking cherries and decided that cherry pies would be a perfect dessert for that evening. Not being quite sure how many cherries she needed for enough pies to feed thirty-six, she bought a rather large bag full of cherries. On our return to Val-Kill, Grandmère rushed into the kitchen to show Marge her prize from the fruit stand.

"Oh, Marge, aren't these cherries beautiful! They'll make such delicious pies for dessert tonight."

Marge stood up, feet planted squarely in the center of the kitchen, put her hands on her hips, locked eyes with my grandmother, and said, "And just who do you think is going to pit all those cherries for your cherry pies?"

Marge often accommodated whatever treasure my grandmother might bring back from the farmers' market, but at this particularly busy time she was not about to stop everything and pit cherries before making three or four pies to feed the large number of guests for dinner that night. Getting the message that Marge was far too busy for this extra task, my grandmother retreated from the kitchen. However, not being willing to forego having cherry pie, later that afternoon, Grandmère enlisted Janet, Maureen Corr, and several of the weekend guests to join my grandmother around the kitchen table and pit cherries. Marge then placed the pitted cherries into her home-made pie shells for delicious cherry pies.

Often Grandmère visited the vegetable stand after church on Sunday. Janet would ride with us, and Grandmère would drop her off at the Catholic church before we proceeded on to Saint James, our Episcopal church. Janet had concluded Reverend Gordon Kidd, the Episcopal rector, was long-winded because she often had a long wait before she was picked up and we all went on to the vegetable stand. Fortunately, Janet usually had the companionship of Maureen Corr, who was also Catholic. Maureen was a hard-working, gentle women blessed with a delicate sense of humor. Janet had a special relationship with Maureen, who was someone with whom she shared her private thoughts and concerns. There is no doubt that Maureen was loved by us all and was willing to mentor us when necessary. She was especially helpful to me as I learned how to handle questions from the press that, at times, were too personal. Being Grandmère's assistant meant that work never ceased. She often was up late typing the "My Day" column or typing responses to my grandmother's voluminous mail. When they traveled, Maureen was known sometimes to type the day's work on her lap while sitting in the bathroom to dull the clacking noise so Grandmère could sleep. Her work and devotion to my grandmother denied her much of a private life. She never married but was devoted to her sister and brother-in-law.

Until my grandfather lost the use of his legs as a result of polio, Grandmère had never had any need to drive a car. But FDR's political dreams would be in question if his name were not kept in public awareness during his efforts to recover. Louis Howe, FDR's close political adviser and friend, convinced Grandmère to tour the state, making speeches and attending political meetings in order to keep in touch with the voters while FDR regained his strength. This meant that Louis Howe had to teach my grandmother to drive. Grandmère conquered many tasks, but driving was one she never mastered.

My Uncle Franklin, an importer of Fiats and Jaguars, could have given my grandmother a "good deal" on a more luxurious car, but being a practical person, Grandmère was content with her small Fiat sedan. Trips with her could be memorable, and on one clear, blue-skied, summer day, when Sally was six and I was ten, Grandmère drove us down our dirt driveway to Route 9G and headed north for the Rhinecliff Bridge. This was a familiar route for Grandmère, who had lived as a child with her grandmother, in Tivoli, New York, several miles north of Rhinecliff. Hollyhocks and roses bloomed beside the houses and barns we passed, and in the pastures dairy cows rhythmically swished their tails to keep the flies away while they ambled along contentedly chewing grass. We approached the bridge, turned left, and suddenly were directly over the wide Hudson River. The dense struts and braces of the bridge made it difficult to see anything except quick glimpses of white sails pulling tiny hulled sailboats behind them and an occasional tugboat pushing long barges as they inched along upriver. I loved to spot the large mansions with graceful green lawns reaching to the edge of the river. These perfectly groomed lawns and large, elegant houses, once the estates of the Hudson River Valley gentry, were now for the most part transformed into convents owned by the Catholic Church.

We crossed the bridge and came to a two-way stop. Grandmère stopped the car and dutifully looked both ways. Seeing that the coast was clear, she put the car in first gear and let the clutch out with a jerk, and the little Fiat stalled. So she put the car in neutral, turned the ignition, gave it some gas, put the clutch in, and shifted into first gear, this time letting the clutch out slowly so the car moved forward. Perhaps assuming that automobiles traveled at the same rate of speed as horse-drawn carriages, Grandmère now did not feel it necessary to look again for any approaching vehicles. Suddenly, I heard the screech of brakes, the blare of a horn, and I spotted a red pickup truck heading for the passenger side of the Fiat. I let out a yelp, which certainly did not help the situation, and Grandmère flinched. For an instant it seemed as if we would be hit, but the truck swerved out in front of us, the driver yelling various indecipherable words and continuing on down the road. Grandmère seemed flustered, but only for a moment. She quickly regained her composure and exclaimed, "Oh, my dear!" as we continued on our way.

Sinking into our seats, Sally and I looked at each other, knowing that we would try not to laugh about this until we got home. At the time, however, we knew better than to act as if anything unusual had happened. Sally and I had developed a ritual while driving with Grandmère—we would fold our hands, pretend to be praying for safe passage, look at each other, and giggle. Usually, Grandmère ignored us. Still, Sally and I did not think Grandmère's driving unique; we assumed all grandmothers drove like ours.

My grandmother's driving technique never improved and caused concern among family members who feared a serious accident. In her early seventies, while driving from Val-Kill to New York City on the Taconic State Parkway, a particularly narrow, winding, four-lane road, Grandmère pulled into the left lane to pass a slower car and, unable to judge the distance between the cars, moved back into the right lane nearly hitting the car she had just passed. To avoid an accident, the other driver slammed on the brakes and swerved onto the shoulder, coming to a sudden stop, just missing bushes and trees. Hearing the screech, Grandmère peered into her rearview mirror and realized her error. She pulled her car over and hurried back to the car behind her to see if the driver was all right. As Grandmère approached, a man emerged from the car. Though somewhat shaken he instantly recognized the woman who had nearly caused a terrible accident. "Oh, Mrs. Roosevelt, I am so sorry," he said.

"I am the one who is sorry," my grandmother replied. "Are you all right?"

"Oh no, I was in your way, Mrs. Roosevelt, I am so sorry, I was in your way."

Grandmère asked the man for his name and address because she planned to write him an apology even though he kept insisting that he had been in her way and their little accident had been completely his fault.

When my grandmother told my father what had happened, he asked for the man's name and address. For several months my father had been trying to convince his mother to hire a chauffeur and to stop driving; clearly, she was a danger to herself as well as others. Daddy thought that if this man would just report this incident to the police, just maybe, he could get her license revoked. Daddy pleaded with the man to report my grandmother's dangerous driving to the police. However, the man held to his story: it was he who'd been in the wrong; he had been in Mrs. Roosevelt's way, and he refused to cooperate with my father. Grandmère continued to drive.

Janet recalls being at the kitchen window watching my grandmother get into her Fiat, backing up in order to turn and drive out of the driveway. In order to turn around, the car had to avoid a tree with a two-foot-high stone wall around its base. For most drivers this would be a simple task, but Janet, knowing otherwise, often watched as Grandmère put the car in reverse, looked over her shoulder, and proceeded to back into the stone wall. Having hit the wall, Grandmère then put the car in gear and drove out the driveway, completely satisfied with her method for navigating obstacles.

Finally, toward the end of her life, Grandmère did give up driving and hired a chauffeur. Archibald Curnan, Charlie Curnan's brother, a kindly, three-hundred-pound man nicknamed "Tubby," became my grandmother's friend and driver. By this time, a Fiat Spider—an even smaller, two-seater, convertible sports car—had replaced the slightly larger Fiat sedan. The new model was not only smaller but quite low to the ground. Tubby would open the car door for her, help her as she started to bend down, steady her while she folded her left leg and lowered her bottom nearly to the ground in order to sit in the passenger seat. Finally, she was able to squeeze her right leg beside her left in the narrow space in front of the seat. Tubby then went around to the driver's side, opened the door, and gazed into the small space into which he had to compress his own huge body. With his characteristic smile and good humor, Tubby let himself down with a thud, tilting the car significantly toward the driver's side. The Fiat's suspension was challenged to keep the car's chassis more than a few inches off the ground. I think my grandmother, having never owned a sports car, actually found the experience to be fun. Whenever the weather permitted, Tubby and Grandmère put the top down, which gave them more room. It always made me smile to see these happy, gray-haired, overweight people tightly fitting into the tiny, snappy, blue-gray sports car as they drove down our dirt lane.

CHAPTER 4

Val-Kill Visitors

The ten bedrooms at Val-Kill were occupied nearly every weekend. Most people wanted to visit during the warm fall and summer months, but weekends during the winter could be busy as well. Grandmère enjoyed being surrounded by friends and family. However, in "Eleanor Roosevelt style," no particular fuss was made about guests no matter how important they might be. Fancy dinnerware was not brought out for special guests. The household routine was the same for kings, queens, important politicians, and ordinary people. Secret Service protection was among the perks available to former First Ladies; however, my grandmother chose to refuse any sort of protection. Security often did accompany some of the dignitaries who visited Val-Kill, however. As children the only way we were certain someone important was coming to visit was by the large entourages accompanying royalty or heads of state. Staff or security assigned to stay with the member of the royal family or head of state were accommodated at Val-Kill, while other members of the retinue were put up in motels in Hyde Park but included in meals at Val-Kill. Regardless of station in life, every visitor was met with Grandmère's sincere broad smile and warm welcome.

The number of expected dinner guests could change at the last minute. On one occasion, Grandmère realized that only thirteen people would be seated at the table. My grandmother's superstition prevailed and she called our house to ask if Sally or I could come for dinner to make the number fourteen. Sally had a school function that evening and I was babysitting. So it was agreed that our youngest sister, Joanie, age three, would attend instead, even though she would be sitting in her high-chair. Grandmère was satisfied as her table was now surrounded by fourteen people, and Marge accordingly found something more appropriate for a three-year-old to eat, despite the fact that Joanie had already had her supper.

Among the royalty that visited Val-Kill, my grandmother's good friend Queen Juliana of the Netherlands came for a weekend in 1952.

APR 7 1952

NEW YORK HERALD TRIBUNE.

Sunday Morning—The Queen Goes to Church

Nat Fein

Queen Juliana of the Netherlands with Mrs. Franklin D. Roosevelt and Mrs. Roosevelt's grand-daughter, Nina, outside St. James Episcopal Church at Hyde Park after the services yesterday

Figure 4.1. Eleanor Roosevelt, Queen Juliana, Nina. *Source*: *New York Herald Tribune*, public domain.

This was the first time I experienced a visit from a member of a royal family. Mostly I remember that she was a person, like my grandmother, who acted so completely naturally that I forgot she was from a long line of formidable royal European leaders. Queen Juliana and my grandmother had become friends not as a Queen and First Lady but as two women who shared concerns for people throughout the world. On the day that the Queen was leaving to go back to New York, she turned to my grandmother and said she'd like to take me back to the Netherlands as my hair and bangs made me look so much like a perfect Dutch girl.

Eight years later, Queen Juliana's eldest child, Princess Beatrix, visited Val-Kill during a tour of the United States. At this time, I was a teenager and only a few years younger than the princess. My grandmother, wanting her to have a good time while she was at Val-Kill, arranged a dinner for the princess, her entourage, and some local dignitaries. Instead of seating her according to protocol at the head table, Grandmère put the princess, my brother, my brother's college roommate David Stein, and me at the children's table. The four of us chatted about school, the hectic itinerary the princess had to endure while on her tour of the U.S., and how much we liked the dessert. Grandmère may have ignored protocol, but this was her house and not a state visit, so she tried to help the princess enjoy a few minutes of talking with people closer to her own age. Princess Beatrix would later succeed her mother and became Queen Beatrix.

Haile Selassie's visit was memorable to me because of the many gifts presented, with formal fanfare, to my grandmother during his short stay. I was about eleven and knew little of the complicated history of Ethiopia, but I remember how its formidable monarch, bearded, with a dark complexion, bowed to my grandmother as he presented her with colorful, handmade carpets, handwoven fabrics, and wooden carvings made by Ethiopian craftsmen. A large burlap sack was also carried by one of Haile

Selassie's attendants and laid at Grandmère's feet. With sweeping motions of his hands, Haile Selassie untied the sack. He folded the burlap back to reveal dark roasted coffee beans. He took a deep breath, with eyes closed, his head gently tilted back as if in reverie—this was a moment of euphoria for him as the smell of the coffee beans filled the room. In an excited voice, Haile Selassie explained to Grandmère that this was just a sample of the four hundred pounds of exquisite coffee beans he had brought her, which she would surely appreciate when she tasted the marvels of Ethiopian coffee.

As soon as Haile Selassie had said his good-byes and left, my grandmother turned to my father and said, "John, won't you see to getting this coffee ground?"

Daddy sighed and agreed, knowing full well he would not only have to arrange for grinding this amount of coffee but would need to find storage while Grandmère figured out to whom she would start giving Ethiopian coffee.

We were rarely told what sort of clothing to wear when people visited Val-Kill. Typically, we wore jeans or shorts except for dinner, church, and special occasions. However, when the Queen Mother of Great Britain visited my grandmother for afternoon tea, Grandmère suggested that blue jeans would not be appropriate. Having known each other for years, the Queen Mother and my grandmother were able to visit one another as friends without the formalities attending royals when representing their country. Seated comfortably with only a handful of guests, it was clear to me that this was a woman with twinkling eyes and a warm demeanor. During this visit to the Stone Cottage, I was responsible for making sure my sister, Joan, wore a dress and was introduced to the Queen Mother. Joan, about three at the time, was completely unimpressed and much more interested in the cakes and cookies that covered the table near the Queen

Figure 4.2. Nina, Joan, Queen Mother, lady-in-waiting. *Source*: personal collection of the author.

Mother. I managed to corral her momentarily to present her to the Queen Mother, during which time Joan never took her eyes off the cookies.

Queen Frederica of Greece visited on a cold day for a luncheon in her honor. Haven and I came into Grandmère's house and put our coats, as we usually did, in one of the bedrooms near the living room where cocktails were being served before luncheon. At eleven years old, I had long braids and was so used to my brother pulling my braid that, when I felt a gentle tug on my braid, I wheeled around and yelled, "Stop it, you idiot!"

Instead of facing my annoying brother, however, I was looking into the kind, smiling face of a woman I had never seen before. Clearly, she enjoyed that I thought my brother had pulled my braid. Haven, with a satisfied grin on his face, left the room.

A few minutes later, when I joined the gathering, my grandmother pulled me to her and said, "Nina, I'd like to introduce you to Queen Frederica."

The queen with a lovely, kind smile said, "Oh, we have already met."

Mortified, I gave a quick curtsy but had no idea what to say.

A few years later, Haven, Sally, and I joined my parents on a goodwill tour of Greece. We sailed on the *Queen Frederica* from New York to Athens, then spent time touring archaeological sites and learning about living on a Greek island, where we did not have running water and the electricity was only available for two hours in the evening. During our visit to Greece, we were invited to lunch with the Greek royal family at their summer residence. The queen, remembering our first interaction, asked me with a warm smile what had happened to my long braids. I probably blushed with embarrassment, but I managed to smile and realize that she did not hold my earlier insolence against me.

૮

Grandmère invited her friend Pauli Murray, along with Pauli's niece, Bonnie, and a few United Nations diplomats to spend an October 1954 weekend at Val-Kill enjoying the fall colors of the Hudson River Valley. Pauli Murray was an activist, civil rights attorney, member of the Commission on the Status of Women, and an Episcopal priest of national stature. Saturday morning's plans included a wreath-laying ceremony, a tour of the FDR Presidential Library and Museum, followed by a picnic lunch at Val-Kill. The guests arrived on Friday night during the tail end of Hurricane Hazel, which had wreaked havoc with high winds and heavy rain that had caused deaths, flooding, and substantial damage south of New York. By the time Ms. Murray and the UN guests reached Val-Kill, even though the electricity was off, they were relieved to be off the narrow, winding roads and safely sitting next to the fireplace. Grandmère showed them to their rooms by candlelight and bid them good night. The storm continued through the night with loud thunder that sounded as if it were rolling around the sky and flashing lightning that made the sky look like blinking lights on a movie theater marquee. The first time I heard such thunder it was scary, but Grandmère made me laugh when she told me that Rip Van Winkle was bowling with his friends between New York City and Albany, with the Hudson River as their bowling alley.

The storm ceased during the night, but our electricity remained off, which meant that water could not be pumped from the well to the house. By Saturday morning, we woke to what seemed like an all-encompassing silence. The sky sparkled like polished crystal, and the chilly air smelled of wet, decaying leaves. Intermittently, the silence was broken by crows calling to one another. My mother and I shared the glistening morning on our screened-in porch at the Stone Cottage with a view of the pond, which had overflowed its banks and partially flooded the lawn. I happily ate cold cereal while my mother complained about the "damn electricity" and not having her coffee. The sound of muffled footsteps leaving Val-Kill caught our attention. We looked up to see my grandmother walking by in her bathrobe and slippers. Not far behind her, in single file, were her guests, led by Pauli, in their bathrobes and slippers, each carrying a neatly folded towel and washcloth over an arm and hands gripping toothbrushes, tubes of toothpaste, and soap. My mother looked quizzically at this mother duck leading her parade. Surely, none of them had expected to be wandering around at this early hour in their nightclothes, breathing the crisp fall air, and heading for a swimming pool! We had stopped cleaning the pool over Labor Day weekend, and now leaves from the nearby maple and sycamore trees lined the pool's bottom, turning the water the color of iced tea. I heard Grandmère assuring her guests, "The pool's water is perfectly safe for washing up."

The expressions on the faces of these dignitaries, from European and African countries, indicated their reluctance to wash their faces and brush their teeth in a swimming pool. After all, they had to maintain some sort of dignity. Having given assurances, Grandmère knelt down next to the water by the shallow end of the pool and began washing her face. She then pulled out her toothbrush, squeezed toothpaste on it, and brushed her teeth. Following Grandmère's example, one by one, these usually pampered diplomats knelt down, tentatively dampened their wash cloths in the water, and proceeded to wash their faces then quickly brush their teeth and spit into the pool. As the last person finished, it was clear that everyone had conquered their discomfort, as they started laughing. With extra-wide smiles and a more pronounced bounce to their steps, Pauli Murray and the other UN guests dutifully followed the mother duck into her house to enjoy a cold breakfast. Pauli Murray later wrote to my grandmother, "What a wonderful weekend it was." It was a morning they would long remember.

It was Grandmère's care for her fragile bed linens, which had been inherited from Sara Delano Roosevelt, that caused her to stop my cousin, Barbara Morgan, and me from playing a trick on a newlywed couple visiting Grandmère. Shortly after their marriage in 1957, Harry Belafonte and his wife, the beautiful dancer Julie Robinson, were staying for a night at Val-Kill on his way to work with some young musicians at the nearby Wiltwyck School. Barbara and I, being young teenagers, decided that newlyweds needed some sort of trick played on them and decided to short-sheet the Belafontes' bed. When we told Grandmère our plan, her eyes twinkled, the wrinkles at the side of her mouth deepened, revealing her large Roosevelt teeth, and she laughed. Still with a broad smile and twinkling eyes, she reconsidered.

"Oh, dear, Mr. Belafonte is tall and I am afraid his feet will poke through my worn-out linen. Couldn't you think up something else? Maybe you could put corn flakes in the bed instead."

Barbara and I were too timid to put many corn flakes in their bed, largely because Marge or Becky, who did the linens and made the beds, might get blamed. We did, however, put enough corn flakes in between the sheets to elicit a reaction, or so we thought. But the only thing the newlyweds commented on at breakfast the next morning was how loud the frog chorus had been.

☙

Among the dignitaries who visited Val-Kill, the 1959 arrival of Premier Nikita Khrushchev of the Soviet Union, his wife Nina, and a large entourage of staff was among the more memorable. Prior to their visit, in order to ensure the Russian leader's safety, a small army of security agents was dispatched to scrutinize every inch of Springwood, Val-Kill Cottage, Stone Cottage, the barn, and all the outbuildings, fields, and two hundred acres of woods surrounding the property. Heavily armed security guards were then strategically placed to stand sentry over the property before and during Khrushchev's visit. In spite of all the security, three of my school friends had no trouble sneaking through the woods to a place where they could get a glimpse of the Soviet leader.

Khrushchev's visit was designed for a morning gathering at Val-Kill followed by a wreath-laying ceremony at the FDR gravesite in Springwood's rose garden. Prior to the formal ceremony, Grandmère intended to serve the Soviet dignitaries some coffee, tea, and pastries after their two-hour drive from New York to Hyde Park. The Cold War loomed as a serious threat to Americans as well as Russians. Tensions were high, and Grandmère was trying to extend her usual warm hospitality.

Marge went to work baking all sorts of goodies for the visit; and Grandmère, wanting to help Marge out, brought pastries from a bakery in New York City. I am not sure if it was Marge or my grandmother, but it was decided to also have some borscht available for the Russian guests. Marge's daughter, Janet, remembers that her father, Les, found a gourmet shop in Poughkeepsie that sold the Eastern European beet soup. When Marge tasted the purchased borscht, however, she immediately refused to serve it and made her own.

The property secured, pastries ordered, homemade borscht on hand, and a specific schedule agreed upon, everything was ready for the several black limousines to arrive at Val-Kill by 9:00 AM. Just before 6:00 AM, Grandmère received a telephone call informing her that the premier and his entourage would expect to be served vodka. Grandmère called my father, waking him at this unusual hour, "John, dear, will you please get enough vodka for about fifty people? Mr. Khrushchev, it seems, likes vodka in the morning." Although Daddy was surprised and not sure where he would find enough vodka at that hour of the morning, he called Charlie. With help from Charlie and Les, enough good quality vodka was available for the Russians.

Time permitted only a brief visit at Val-Kill for the entourage before going to the FDR Presidential Library and Museum for the formal wreath-laying ceremony in the Rose Garden. It was a jovial and friendly visit; the Cold War was definitely left

Figure 4.3. Nikita and Nina Khrushchev visit FDR's grave. *Source*: FDR Library, public domain.

behind for a brief while. Mrs. Khrushchev spoke little English but immediately smiled and tried to talk with me when she learned that we had the same first name, Nina.

My mother explained to her that I had gotten the name from a secret service officer of Russian descent. When I was an infant, he referred to me as "Ninishka." The agent was responsible for protecting my father and his family during FDR's presidency. Shortened to Nina, this became the name that was used by the rest of the family and friends, even though my given name is Anne, after my mother.

Trying to stay on schedule, Premier Khrushchev's departure was a bit hectic. The large Russian entourage poured out of Grandmère's front door and hurriedly got into one of the waiting limousines that then had to turn around in a very narrow space. The confusion of how to execute these maneuvers in a dignified fashion seemed to confuse the entire Russian delegation. There was lots of hand-waving and barked directions, but eventually they all seemed to be ready to file out in the proper order toward their next stop. As Premier Khrushchev left the house, he grabbed the largest roll he could find, hurriedly climbed into his limousine, waved the breakfast roll in his hand, a wide grin and a twinkle in his eye, and said to the gathered press and photographers, "One for the road!"

I was too young to appreciate Josh White, who came to Val-Kill at a time when my grandmother was out of town. Josh White had performed at the White House during the time FDR was president, and a friendship began between him and my grandparents, both of whom admired his music and his dedication to civil rights. This well-known singer, songwriter, and civil rights activist was also the brother of Grandmère's assistant, William White, who had been so kind to me when I had polio. While FDR was alive, Josh White had made many visits to Springwood and continued to visit my grandmother at Val-Kill after my grandfather's death. On this memorable occasion, when Josh White came to visit his brother, William, I wandered into the kitchen and was surprised to see a group of people playing guitars and singing. It turned out that Josh, William, and his family members had gathered in the kitchen for a jam session with obvious enjoyment. As unsophisticated as I was at ten years old, I knew this was music to remember.

Even though I do not remember Bernard Baruch spending the night at Val-Kill, he was a well-known presence to all. Statesman, financier, philanthropist, and also a friend and admirer of my grandmother, Mr. Baruch frequently sent goodies from the fanciest pastry shops in New York City. Grandmère would put these in silver candy dishes throughout the house. As children, we liked all the cookies as long as they were not flavored with any alcohol. It so happened that rum cookies were popular gifts from Mr. Baruch. At one point, being very disrespectful, we asked Grandmère if she would ask Mr. Baruch not to send rum cookies but some other kind. Grandmère just smiled at us and said the treats had been sent to her, not to us, and she appreciated the kindness Mr. Baruch had shown her.

A few visitors to Val-Kill were there on a more consistent basis. On many weekends and most holidays, Joe and Trude Lash stayed with Grandmère. Joe, active in student movements, founder of Americans for Democratic Action (a progressive, anti-communist group), and later an assistant editor at the *New York Post* and author of biographies about my grandmother's life, had a long, close, relationship with Grandmère. Prior to his second marriage, to Edna, David Gurewitsch brought his daughter, Grania, for weekend visits. Once David and Edna were married, all three of them continued to be a part of our family gatherings. I don't think we had a holiday without the Lashes, Gurewitsches, or any friend of Grandmère's who didn't have a place to go for the holiday.

Some friends stayed at Val-Kill in times of need and remained for long periods. Lorena Hickock was a formidable, groundbreaking journalist who had written compelling articles and was the first female to have a byline with the Associated Press. "Hick," as she was called, became a friend of my grandmother's and taught her a great deal about the power of the press.

They traveled together extensively to places like the mine country in West Virginia, where Hick demonstrated how press reporting could bring the daily struggles endured by many Americans to the attention of the larger public. Grandmère and Hick offered female journalists access to the White House and elevated women in the male-dominated profession. At some point, the editors from AP and some government advisers to the president became concerned that their close relationship endangered Hick's journalistic objectivity. She resigned from the AP and ended her twenty-year career. My grandmother remained loyal, gave her a place to stay at Val-Kill, and eventually found her a home of her own in Hyde Park.

Figure 4.4. Lorena Hickock. *Source*: FDR Library, public domain.

The Entrup family remembered Hick fondly as one of the more distinctive visitors. Janet, who spent a good deal of time with Hick, remembers that "at first I was a little afraid of her as she seemed so gruff. As I got to know her a little better, I realized she was very kind, intelligent, and so interesting." Often Hick stayed at Val-Kill for weeks at a time whether my grandmother was there or not. As children we interacted with Hick as just another guest, but this guest was different from most of the Val-Kill guests in the way she comported herself and how she dressed.

Janet often went with her father, Les, to Hyde Park to give Hick (who did not have a car) a ride so that she could see her doctor or run errands. Janet remembers that she would be wearing khaki pants, work boots, and a T-shirt with her Camel cigarettes in the pocket. My own memory of Hick only adds the Camel cigarette perpetually hanging out of the corner of her mouth. Janet further remembers that my grandmother once told Hick that there were special people coming to visit Val-Kill and she had to be sure to dress nicely and please wear a bra!

Because Hick spent considerable time at Val-Kill, I got to know and appreciate her better than the short-term guests. As a co-conspirator, I found I could count on Hick to keep me out of trouble. When Hick saw me enjoying a beer with friends at a local bar, she knew I was not of legal drinking age. The bartender was someone I had known in town for years. He probably knew I was only seventeen, and three months shy of the legal drinking age, but discreetly did not ask my age. Hick not only did not say anything to the bartender but also did not say anything to my parents.

I wish I had been wise enough to ask Hick about her life and struggles as a female journalist. I also remember Hick's ability to get to the core of an issue. If any of my cousins or siblings were discussing an issue with the idealism of youth, Hick would quickly ask a question which made us realize we did not really know what we were talking about. Similarly, she would often interject her dry humor, which sometimes would take a few minutes to sink in before I started to laugh. Like so many of Grandmère's friends, Hick came from a completely different background. She was born into poverty, struggled to get an education, and continued to fight gender bias throughout her career. Yet the two women found much in common and forged a true friendship.

℮

Charles Purcell, a struggling actor who made my grandmother laugh, was a friend of hers who often spent much of the summer at Val-Kill. Charles, a colleague of Gore Vidal, who also visited Val-Kill as a friend of Grandmère's, joined Gore in trying to keep the Hyde Park Playhouse, a summer theater, running smoothly. It was Charles who arranged for me to be hired for a summer job at the Playhouse. I don't know how old Charles was when he died, but I was in my teens and my grandmother and I went to his funeral to pay our respects. With sadness in her voice, Grandmère said that she always felt sadder when she confronted the death of a young person.

℮

Uncle David Gray was a favorite among the family members who visited every summer.

He was born in Buffalo, New York, in 1870 and graduated from Harvard in 1892. Prior to becoming the United States ambassador to Ireland in 1940, he had served in France as a member of the American Expeditionary Forces during World War I and later received a doctor of letters from Bowdoin College. Uncle David had married my grandmother's aunt, Maude Hall, a younger sister of Anna Hall Roosevelt, Grandmère's mother. Aunt Maude and her sisters had dazzled New York society at the turn of the century with their beauty and gaiety. I never knew Aunt Maude except through Uncle David's stories about how soft-spoken, yet resolute, she was.

I can still vividly see Uncle David sitting erect in a ladder-backed chair, his thinning wisps of white hair lying in straight

Figure 4.5. David Gray, Eleanor Roosevelt, and Charles Purcell. *Source*: FDR Library, public domain.

lines across his shiny head, his long arms with thin, aristocratic fingers gently resting over the curve of his walking stick. Uncle David always dressed in a coat with a perfectly tied bow tie balanced at his neck. Grandmère insisted that he stay at Val-Kill for at least a month during the summer, exchanging the heat and humidity of his Florida home for that of the Hudson River Valley. Widowed for many years, I think Uncle David adored Aunt Maude but, as he explained it, after her death he had to focus on another mistress to stay alive. A *mistress*—at his age! I could not imagine his perfectly tailored clothes ever being rumpled in a steamy romantic liaison. Uncle David was ninety-eight when he died, but I first knew him as a still-handsome, active, eighty-two-year-old. He regaled us with stories of ladies living nearby in Siesta Key, Florida, knitting him socks and flirting with him. I later learned that, when he talked about "attending to his mistress" with a twinkle in his eye, he was really referring to writing his memoirs about having spent many years in Ireland as the U.S. ambassador. Uncle David admitted that he didn't want to finish his book because it would certainly be the end not only of the book but of his life as well.

As Grandmère's uncle, David treated her as if she, unlike himself, was too old to know what was really going on in the world. At the dinner table, Uncle David took great pleasure in asking a pithy question of those around him while he waited patiently for someone to begin tackling an answer. If Grandmère spoke up, Uncle David would turn to her and say, "Eleanor, quiet, you're too old to know what is going on. I want to hear what the young people think."

Grandmère kept right on talking, which gave us a chance to figure out what Uncle David was getting at. We carefully gathered our own thoughts before engaging in a discussion with a man who spoke several languages, could quote passages from poetry and literature, and who enjoyed playing devil's advocate. Uncle David had lived through, lived in, and lived with most of the recent history that had shaped our lives. One of my cousins, of whom Uncle David was particularly fond, was Chris Roosevelt. Uncle David recognized in Chris a wonderful sense of humor and a lively intelligence. Showing his affection, Uncle David loved to ask Chris to get one thing or another for him, mostly so he could keep Chris on his toes.

At ninety-two, Uncle David decided it was time to embrace God and went through confirmation as an Episcopalian. As a new convert, he relentlessly pushed all of us to attend church regularly and to watch our behavior. I had been attending St. James Episcopal Church, where we even had our own family pew, fairly regularly with my grandmother. My parents, however, believed in the church of the outdoors and rarely attended church except for weddings and funerals. Uncle David kept telling us that we were going to "meet our maker" and would have to atone for our sins. My mother responded, "Uncle David, you waited until you were ninety-two to get confirmed and to atone for at least eighty years of sin—I think I'll wait a while too." Grandmère, on hearing my mother, grinned and reminded Uncle David that there was nothing worse than a suddenly religious convert. I can still hear Uncle David laughing heartily and telling us that the least we could do was to pray for one another. Uncle David said on many occasions, "I am sure to go to heaven because that must be where Maude is."

One of Uncle David's beliefs was that a daily glass of carrot juice kept him healthy. Carrot juice was not something readily available, so Marge, who adored Uncle David, made him fresh carrot juice each day. She also made certain that Uncle David had all the foods he most liked and would remind my grandmother to include dishes for Uncle David during the planning of meals for the week.

At his age travel was cumbersome, but Uncle David had friends in Massachusetts whom he wanted to visit in the sum-

Figure 4.6. David Gray's ninety-second birthday. *Source*: Entrup family personal collection.

mer of 1960. Les agreed to drive Uncle David to Winchester, Massachusetts, combining it with a stay in Boston with Marge and Janet. Unfortunately, their plans were thwarted. After leaving Uncle David with his friends, they were unable to find suitable accommodations in Boston, so they drove back to Hyde Park, making for a very long day. Always thoughtful, Uncle David sincerely appreciated the willingness of the Entrups to drive him the two hundred miles to see his friends. Uncle David wrote Marge and Les a thank-you note and continued to comment to others about the kindness they had shown him and how much he enjoyed their company on the trip to Massachusetts.

ℰ

Of the visitors who were entertained regularly at Val-Kill, Laura Delano, FDR's first cousin, was peerless. Laura Delano, or Aunt

Figure 4.7. Laura Delano ("Aunt Polly"). *Source*: FDR Library, public domain.

Polly, as we called her, lived nearby in Rhinebeck with her champion Irish Setters and Long-Haired Dachshunds.

Aunt Polly was witty, warm, and full of humorous stories. During some of the most stressful times of his presidency, FDR relied on Aunt Polly's company for relaxation. She often joined him for cocktails and meals in the White House and was at his side when he died in Warm Springs, Georgia. Well-known in the world of judging and showing champion dogs, Aunt Polly's show dogs, like their owner, lived pampered lives. This energetic, tiny-framed woman, not even five feet tall, dyed her hair purple as soon as she noticed her first grey hair. Initially, a small widow's peak was drawn, also purple, forming a painted triangle from her hairline in the center of her forehead to a point about half an inch toward her nose. With age her purple widow's peak grew larger and more prominent. When I asked my mother why a never-married woman would draw a widow's peak on her forehead, I was told that Aunt Polly had been in love with a close relative of Emperor Hirohito, and being neither Japanese nor royalty, marriage would never be permitted. Returning from Japan before World War II war broke out, Aunt Polly felt as if she had been widowed. This story may have been apocryphal, but it certainly made Aunt Polly more eccentric.

Aunt Polly's unusual hair color was second only to the amount of jewelry, glittering diamonds, rubies, sapphires, and emeralds with which she covered her body and clothes. It occurred to me as a ten-year-old that her jewelry may have weighed more than she did. I had never seen such a display, nor had I ever encountered such an unusual woman, who may have been small in stature but was anything but diminutive. My grandmother and Aunt Polly were bound by years of shared experiences that bind family members even if they are quite different. Never without an opinion about government officials, Aunt Polly's sense of humor kept everyone, including my grandmother, laughing.

My parents, Haven, and I were often invited to Aunt Polly's house for dinner or to endure her freezing cold, spring-fed swimming pool.

Figure 4.8. Thanksgiving at Val-Kill. Front row: Barbara Morgan, Frank, Chris, Haven; second row: Laura Delano (Aunt Polly), Eleanor Roosevelt, Sally, Nina; back row: John, Anne, Sue, Franklin Jr., Minnewa, Elliott. *Source*: Elliott/Roosevelt family personal collection.

I always looked forward to the dinner occasions, especially as a teenager when I had overcome my shyness around adults. The rooms in Aunt Polly's house were arranged to be proportionate to her size. This was a woman who would not be swallowed up by expansive, spacious rooms. The living room, even though fairly large, was arranged to make it look small. Two pairs of comfortable chairs were placed facing each other on either side of the fireplace. A small table placed between each pair of chairs and a butler's table in the center allowed four people to sit close to one another. Additional chairs, artfully scattered around the rest of the room, could be arranged, if necessary, to accommodate more than four people. Arriving at the front door, we were always met by the housekeeper, who ushered us into this cozy setting for cocktails before dinner. Once her guests were settled, Aunt Polly made her grand entrance. She would glide into the room, complete with jewelry jangling from her wrists, and followed by at least two dogs, each with a diamond or sapphire clasp affixed to its gleaming coat. Typically, she wore some sort of colorful, silk pantsuit with matching silk slippers on her tiny feet. On one occasion, my mother commented on Aunt Polly's beautiful white silk outfit, and Aunt Polly, with great pleasure, said, "I bought this to be buried in. I want to wear it so I am used to it, since I have to wear it for eternity."

Later in her life Aunt Polly became fascinated with a particularly disagreeable Pekingese dog. By that time, when we joined her for dinner, Aunt Polly made her grand entrance holding this bejeweled puff of threat. Aunt Polly would then place him, growling, on a marble table next to her chair and the chair next to hers. Fearing this disagreeable dog, as soon as the housekeeper opened the front door, Haven and I ran into the living room to grab a chair as far as possible from the marble table and the disagreeable pet. Unfortunately, it was usually I who had not managed to get into a safe seat and had to sit next to this snapping, snarling piece of cream-colored fluff. No matter how I tried, I could never get used to the prized Pekingese's growl every time I so much as shifted in my chair. Aunt Polly, without concern, pointed out all the places where her "wonderful baby" had bitten her.

There were, however, occasions when visitors to Val-Kill were not quite so welcome. My grandmother did not have any sort of security detail or Secret Service protection. Upon leaving the White House, my grandmother felt it unnecessary for the American people's tax dollars to be spent protecting her. The only "perk" my grandmother retained was a stamp of her signature that allowed her to mail letters for free instead of using a three-cent stamp.

On one of the quieter nights at Val-Kill—my grandmother was away and my parents were in the city—only Haven and I were in the Stone Cottage. Charlie Curnan came to the door at about

10:00 at night holding his shotgun. Startled, Haven and I asked what was going on when Charlie, in his calm, yet serious tone, told us that there was a call from the owner of a bar in Hyde Park who had overheard a customer bragging that he was going to get rid of all those "damn Roosevelts." Apparently, this particular person then brandished his pistol and continued to rant about how all the Roosevelts and their friends should be in their graves. Charlie told me to get my shotgun, load it, and sit facing one of the doors to our house while Haven, with his loaded shotgun, was stationed at another door. My father had taught Haven and me how to handle guns in our early teens and had given me a 20-gauge shotgun for Christmas. We were instructed to shoot for the legs just to stop this apparently inebriated man if he managed to get into the house. Charlie was going to alert the people staying at my grandmother's house, and he would stay there assuming our drunken assailant would most surely go to my grandmother's house first. In the meantime, the police had been alerted and actually intercepted the inebriated man in the town of Hyde Park. Haven and I sat, waiting until past midnight until we were notified that all was well.

Val-Kill was only a short distance from the state hospital, where people resided who had been diagnosed with a variety of mental illnesses. Occasionally, patients would wander away and end up at our house. On one occasion, Janet was walking out of the lane toward Route 9G when a man jumped out of the bushes and demanded that she take him to see Mrs. Roosevelt. A terrified Janet ran back to her house. From then on Marge insisted that Les needed to drive Janet so that she would not be on the long driveway by herself. On the couple of occasions that someone actually knocked on our door insisting that they were here on official business, my father would invite them in and quietly call the hospital staff while we served coffee and some cookies to our new guest. Other than being unsettling, these visits did not cause any harm.

Christmastime at Val-Kill was magical and full of family and friends for every meal.

Figure 4.9. Christmas chaos. Background: Elliott cousins. foreground: Eleanor Roosevelt II, Anne, Eleanor Roosevelt, Sally. *Source*: Elliott/ Roosevelt family personal collection.

Grandmère had a closet upstairs at Val-Kill where she hid gifts she purchased throughout the year for the many people to whom she gave Christmas presents. Surely, Grandmère knew that the children were aware of this secret closet and periodically checked to see what we might be getting for Christmas. Janet remembers how exciting it was to help wrap all the presents and how many there were. Every Christmas, Grandmère held a Christmas party for families that had worked for her mother-in-law at Springwood or had worked for her at Val-Kill. Each person was given a gift—the men always got a tie from Arnold Constable (a department store in New York), and the women received a purse from the same store. All the children were given large cornucopias filled with Christmas candies. It was a festive event with tea, juice for the children, Christmas cookies, and colorfully decorated cakes.

On Christmas Eve Grandmère always read Dickens's *A Christmas Carol* to us. After a roast beef dinner, everyone gathered in the living room by the fire with the twinkling Christmas tree in the background.

Figure 4.10. Val-Kill Christmas, Joan in foreground. *Source*: Elliott/ Roosevelt family personal collection.

Coffee was served and we all settled comfortably while my grandmother pulled out her worn copy of Dickens's beloved work and began reading to us.

For many years Haven and I started in the late fall to gather enough pine cones from the woods to fill a large basket to give to Grandmère for Christmas. In the basement of the Stone Cottage, we painted each pine cone with model airplane glue in a variety of colors and sprinkled them with sparkling glitter. When the pine cones were put into the fireplace they burned and danced with a wonderful array of colors.

The center of the dining room table was always decorated with creative Christmas scenes.

Figure 4.11. Val-Kill Christmas table. *Source*: Elliott/Roosevelt family personal collection.

One Christmas the center of the table was covered with cotton to represent snow. Small trees, greenery, and various Christmas decorations including a nativity scene were artfully placed among the fluffy cotton. When we all came to the table for lunch and found our seats, both my father and Uncle Franklin brought their pre-luncheon martinis and their cigarettes with them. Suddenly one of the cigarettes caught the cotton-snow on fire. Everyone at the table, it seems, erupted in gasps, but my father and his brother, determined to save the day, threw their martinis on the fire. It was eventually extinguished through more thoughtful approaches. Instead of being horrified, my grandmother just took all this chaos in stride and was quite relieved that very little was actually burned.

Our Christmas dinner included two turkeys, stuffing, cranberry sauce, green beans, mashed potatoes, and creamed onions, along with various other side dishes that Marge enjoyed making. My father and my Uncle Franklin each carved a turkey, continuing their childhood competitions to see whose carving of one of the two turkeys was the most professional. The meal concluded with an assortment of traditional pies—pumpkin, mincemeat, and apple.

CHAPTER 5

Campobello

Our Beloved Island

Before I was old enough to have a summer job, I remember standing by the screen door of the Stone Cottage, like a racing colt in the starting gate, waiting for the signal to get into our sleek, shiny, black Buick sedan. I had packed my small blue suitcase with blue jeans, shirts, a sweater, sneakers, underwear, hairbrush, a toothbrush, and a bathing suit in case it was hot enough to swim. My mother, father, Sally, Haven, my cousin Stewart Elliott, and I were all going to spend two weeks on Campobello, the island where generations of my maternal and paternal families had summered to escape the heat of Boston, New York, and Washington, D.C. Going to Campobello was the only trip we took as a family. Typically, our visits were arranged to coincide with visits to the island by my grandmother. Grandmère's niece, Ellie Elliott, and her children often joined us for brief periods as well.

In order to get to Campobello Island, we needed to arrive at the ferry landing in Lubec, Maine, before the man operating the ferry (a small barge that carried a couple of cars across the narrows to the Canadian island of Campobello) tied up for the night. This meant we had to leave Hyde Park at dawn. No amount of cajoling, generous tipping, or begging could persuade the ferryman to operate one minute after 5:00 PM.

My parents, not known for cheery morning attitudes, grunted, letting a few swear words fly as they hastily jammed suitcases, extra coats, books, boots, and rain gear into the not-very-large trunk of our car. My cousin, sister, brother, and I put ourselves in a suspended state, walking quietly, not asking any questions, and staying as far away from them as possible until we climbed elbow to elbow into the back seat and headed for what we considered to be an idyllic, if fog-bound, island. Grand-mère, joined us later, accompanied by Tubby or Joe and Trude Lash.

One part of the trip I looked forward to was our routine stop for lunch in Maine. While my siblings ordered lobster, I loved the steamed clams. Daddy brought a large thermos into the restaurant and quietly put it on the floor beside his feet. He and Mother then ordered a glass of ice with their lobsters. Surely no one was fooled that the clear liquid they poured over the ice was water. No road trip lunch in Maine was complete without a martini (or two). We knew that after lunch our father's driving on the narrow two-lane roads through northern Maine would be faster and bumpier.

At the dock, gulls sent piercing darts of sound toward the fishermen for not sharing a few morsels of their meager day's catch. We hurriedly drove onto the elderly, dilapidated ferry and watched as the tide began its famous rapid rise of nearly forty feet, causing the water to lap hungrily against the creosote-soaked wooden pilings, sealed against the elements by layers of bird droppings. The ferryman, recognizing my father, went through the exact same routine Daddy had heard for years. "John—good ta see ya!" Then after a pause his smile broadened, and with twinkling eyes he continued, "I remember the time when your father was president and he brought a destroyer through these narrows—scared the shit outta us."

Upon disembarking, there was a short drive from the island landing to the rounded, barn-shaped, red-shingled Campobello cottage.

Its dark green shutters blended into the tall pine trees that graced each side of the house. Even with a gray evening

Figure 5.1. Roosevelt Cottage, Campobello, Canada. *Source*: New Brunswick Tourism via Wikimedia Commons.

mist beginning to blanket the house, I was excited—this was an inviting house, well worn by years of young and old Roosevelts who spent their summers here. I loved being here. In my great grandparents' day, wealthy families from Boston and New York frequented Campobello, where they played tennis, sailed in the icy waters of Passamaquoddy Bay, and kept household staff busy with a succession of lunch and dinner parties. Now the island was mostly inhabited by the families connected in some way to the fishing industry and only a few others who came for the summer.

The Roosevelt Cottage was built in 1897 for the Kuhn family from Massachusetts. Mrs. Kuhn's will stipulated that the cottage should be sold to Sara Delano Roosevelt, who owned the cottage next door. Mrs. Kuhn was fond of Sara and my grandparents and wanted them to eventually occupy the house. Sara's cottage, which was not large enough to accommodate her growing family, was sold when Sara purchased the Kuhn property as a belated wedding gift for her son and daughter-in-law. Sara's cottage eventually burned down. With thirty-four rooms and two bathrooms, this "cottage" gave ample space for the five children, their friends, family, and the many guests who would enjoy this idyllic spot over the years. The Calder family, longtime residents of Campobello Island, looked after the family while my grandparents were in Campobello and took care of the house after everyone left at the end of the summer. At FDR's death, Victor and Armand Hammer purchased the house. The Hammers were close friends of the family and insisted on keeping everything much the same way it was when my grandparents enjoyed their summers there. Victor and his wife, Irene, spent time during the summer months on the island and invited my parents, grandmother, and my cousin Ellie Roosevelt Elliott to come every summer and to "bring all the children." We loved being with the Hammers who often entertained us. Victor would play his guitar while Irene sang songs from her time as a professional performer. We played games of charades with lots of laughter, and everyone took turns acting out the phrases. We all wanted Grandmère on our team, as she recognized the phrases quickly. The Hammers did not plan any extra social events, ensuring that my grandmother could relax and enjoy her stay.

In fifty years, little had changed in the house. Water was still gravity fed from a large wooden water tower that stood next to the house; an old-fashioned water heater stood in the kitchen and warmed us on chilly mornings.

Like most kitchens of its era, there was a long work table in the center, a breakfast nook next to a window looking out toward the front lawn, large tubs for washing dishes, and an old-fashioned wood- or coal-fired stove. Upstairs the bedrooms had simple, painted wooden furniture and soft, well-worn cotton comforters over woolen blankets that smelled of mothballs. Model boats and airplanes my father and Uncle Franklin made as children still hung from the ceiling in the room they had shared. Downstairs, the living room was in the center of the house with the dining room and kitchen on one side. The other side had been used as office and parlor space for FDR so that he could continue working while vacationing. His office was furnished with

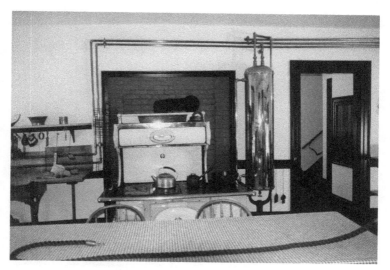

Figure 5.2. Campobello kitchen. *Source*: Photo by Nick Gibson, personal collection of the author.

creaking wicker furniture that had been there for years, and rag rugs covered the wooden floors. His desk looked as if he would be right back to finish some paperwork, and his telescope still stood by the window, pointed toward the bay so that he could identify boats sailing by and watch the whales as they played in the deep cold water of the bay.

Returning to Campobello several years ago with our children, the island seemed much the same to me. The ferry has been replaced by a bridge from Lubec, making it easier for tourists to reach the island and for the islanders to access the mainland. The Roosevelt Cottage is well cared for, but perhaps it is a combination of the smells and sounds that make the house different. I missed the scattered books and unfinished puzzles in the corner of the living room. Old wicker furniture no longer groans and pops with people sitting in them. The blueberry bushes that reached from the porch nearly to the beach are now gone, replaced by a well-manicured lawn.

Figure 5.3. View from the porch. *Source*: Photo by Nick Gibson, personal collection of the author.

Our time in Campobello was filled with daylong fishing trips, clamming, picking blueberries, eating lobsters, and at least one day when we ventured by boat north and east across the Passamaquoddy Bay to the quaint Canadian fishing village of St. Andrews, New Brunswick. Mother loved to shop in the stores filled with British goods, English china, tartan kilts, cashmere sweaters, and hand-spun yarns.

If we were lucky and had a particularly hot day, Harry Matin, a next-door neighbor and owner of a sardine factory on Campobello, would invite us to swim in his swimming pool. Few people were brave enough to swim in the water surrounding the island. It was so cold that the fishermen never learned to swim, as they said that upon ending up in the water, swimming would only prolong an inevitable death. In conspiratorial voices they told us the story of a teenage boy who tried to swim across the bay but had only lasted for five minutes before drowning.

Because the house was similar to a living museum—the famous people were gone now, but the house remained as if they had just stepped out for a moment—my sister, Sally, and I decided to become tour guides. On rainy days, restless after playing Monopoly, hearts, crazy eights, and pounce, Sally and I put a sign in front of the house: OPEN FOR TOURS—25 CENTS. We assumed we would have a small market, as we had seen people occasionally stop across the street to take pictures. Much to our delight, a few people happily paid our entrance fee. We identified ourselves as summer guests named Nina and Sally. Occasionally our professionalism would falter, and we would refer to the time "our grandmother lived here." Once, in the excited state of being a tour guide, I let slip that I was staying in the same room my Aunt Anna had used as a child and, "Nothing has been changed—not even the quilt." In order to answer questions, Sally and I quickly learned as much as we could about the function of each room during the time of our grandparents.

Thoroughly into our roles and without regard for the privacy of the people, including our parents, Sally and I took our tours upstairs to show off the beautiful view from the bedrooms that overlooked Friars Bay. Without knocking, we opened doors and proudly exhibited the two small bathrooms on the second floor with the claw-footed bathtubs and pull-chain toilets. Once, as we opened the door to one of the bedrooms, we interrupted our mother while she was changing her clothes. With a shriek, she dove into the closet, and we hurried our tour downstairs to avoid further drama and subsequent rebuke.

Sally and I soon realized we had started a business that could potentially make—by our standards—a lot of money. I am proud to say that, at the outset of the Sally and Nina Tours, we decided to donate the proceeds to the library in Campobello's main town of Welch Pool to purchase more books for children. As eager as we were to make money, we only guided tours on rainy days when there was nothing else to do and when Grandmère was not there. Without being told not to, we realized that while Grandmère may not have minded, the tours would have given her less time to enjoy a few days of quiet relaxation.

When the weather permitted, we fished from the Hammers' small fishing boat, typical of the boats owned by the local fishermen, with a small cabin, covered bow to shield the captain during rough weather, and an open stern. Besides a built-in wooden bench that also served as a storage chest for additional gas tanks, there were a couple of folding aluminum chairs and a small grill in the stern. We used the grill to cook our usual lunch of hot dogs and toasted buns. The adults relaxed, watching the rippling blue waters or reading a book while we fished.

When Grandmère was with us, she sat in the stern, reading a book or knitting. To ward off the chilly air, she bundled up in a sweater, heavy stockings, and a jacket with a scarf covering her hair. Every time we caught a fish, our shrieks of joy were acknowledged with a nod of her head and a smile. In her August 11, 1959, "My Day" column, Grandmère wrote, "[T]he fog cleared sufficiently so that all the young people went deep-sea fishing. My granddaughter, Nina, caught the biggest pollock, weighing 10 pounds. Everyone was busy pulling up smaller pollock and cod, so I think chowder will be the order of the day for some time to come."

Watching the whales play was the most exciting part of our summer boating experiences. Mostly finback and minke whales came to feed and mate in the latter part of the summer, and we were mesmerized by the way they rose out of the water in shining splendor, raising their huge bodies far above us in our small fishing boat before diving back in, only to surface again like a puppy dancing for a treat. We had been told to always keep the engine running so that the whales would hear us and not accidentally crush us as they dove back into the water.

Almost every day, Grandmère gathered all the children, each toting baskets or paper bags, and led us into the blueberry thicket on the back of the house, facing the bay, to pick enough berries for the cook to make pies for dinner. Grandmère loved the fresh blueberries from Campobello and northern Maine and took delight in picking as many as were necessary for the day. I never learned to pick blueberries without turning my clothes blue-black, but Grandmère deftly picked them much faster than we did and never seemed to stain her clothes. After the blueberries were washed, Grandmère patiently showed us how to use plain soap and a scrub brush to rid our fingers of the dark blue stains. It never seemed to work very well. Our fingers were blue for days.

At low tide, Grandmère took us to her favorite clamming cove. The first time I went clamming, I stood entranced, watching Grandmère push her long, crooked toes into a bubble in the sand as the wave receded from the shore. She bent down and dug as fast as she could with her beautifully manicured, polished fingers to dig out a large steamer! When the wave curled back around her bare feet, Grandmère picked up her skirts and headed for the dry, still-cold sand to wait for the next time the water receded, exposing bubbles in the sand which signaled the presence of more clams. Awkward at first, I was not as quick, but eventually got the hang of it. I remember being very excited as our bucket filled with clams—steamed clams were my favorite! Grandmère always gathered more than the rest of us, but Sally and I had so much fun it was hard to decide if we wanted to fish or to go clamming with our expert grandmother.

Grandmère made a point of visiting Mrs. Calder, who had been my grandparents' housekeeper when the family was staying at the house in Campobello. By the time I was going to the island, Mrs. Calder had retired, but I enjoyed our visits and listening to my grandmother assure Mrs. Calder that the "children" (my aunt, uncles, and father) were well and happy. Mrs. Calder had known the family for many years, and we always paid our respects to this hardworking and gracious lady. When I returned to Campobello with my children years later, Mrs. Calder was in a rest home and frail. Seeing me brought a sparkle to her eyes and a broad smile as she remembered the time with my family for so many years.

In those days, an activity-filled summer day at Campobello would end with all of us gathered on the long porch overlooking the bay for cocktails and juice. Grandmère rocked slowly in a wooden rocking chair and knitted while she watched the sky change from shades of blue to orange, and the sun sank into the cold waters of Friars Bay. For her, Campobello held memories of a carefree life with her children when they were young, as well as life-changing memories of her husband having been stricken with polio and taken off the island on a stretcher, never to walk again without aid. Notwithstanding the tragedy that crippled FDR, Grandmère found Campobello, as she found Val-Kill, a place of renewal and peace.

CHAPTER 6

Travels with Grandmère

Leningrad

Sept 13, 1958

Dearest Nina,

We are getting much more attention this time and seeing all we ask to see. The only thing I can't find is emotionally disturbed, delinquent children but tomorrow morning we drive into the country to some children's sanatoriums and I may find these answer my question.

I hope all at home are well and that you have had a good semester. Would you like to come on a trip sometime if Mummy and Daddy would let you?

Good luck in school this year. I hope you come home for Thanksgiving.

Much love

Grandmère

By the end of 1958, the country was in turmoil. Newspapers in the U.S. were filled with stories about the launch of *Sputnik*, and

Americans worried about the Soviet Union's emergence as a rival superpower. Federal troops were being deployed in Little Rock, Arkansas, to enforce school desegregation. I had just turned sixteen, a junior in high school, and I was at Val-Kill for the holidays.

When my grandmother took my hand a couple of days after Christmas, she explained that she had my parents' permission to ask me something important. "Nina, dear," she said, "how would you like to go with me to visit Aunt Anna in Iran and meet my friend David Ben-Gurion in Israel?"

Unprepared for this request, my heart sank as I realized I would not be able to go with her. "Oh, no," I said, "the head mistress of my school would never let me out unless it was the summer break."

But Grandmère, with a broad smile, replied, "I've already talked with Miss Fitch, and she thinks it would be just fine for you to miss a few weeks of school during your spring holiday." Without my knowledge, Grandmère had spoken with the head of my school to request that I be excused for about six weeks during the coming spring term so that I could accompany her on a trip that would include Turkey, Iran, Israel, Italy, France, and England.

I don't know why Grandmère chose to take me with her on this trip. Haven and my cousin John Boettiger had gone with Grandmère to Europe a couple of years earlier, and perhaps it was simply that she knew I was interested in places I had never seen. I often asked Grandmère about her travels and loved the stories of elephants in India, exotic villages in Africa, and her descriptions of European cities. During her travels, Grandmère took the time to send me postcards with notes about what she was seeing. She once told me the story of an African village she visited where the women lined up on the landing strip to greet her upon her arrival. Typically, these villagers covered themselves from the waist down. It had been suggested to the women that they should cover their tops when greeting their distinguished guest, as she was a woman who wore clothes that covered her from her shoulders to below her knees. As soon as the women saw Grandmère step from the plane onto the ground and walk toward her hostesses, the women in unison raised their skirts to cover their breasts, leaving the rest of their bodies exposed.

The idea of traveling with my grandmother on any trip overwhelmed me with excitement. For the next two and a half months, I had a perpetual smile. However, mixed with the anticipation of such an adventure was the fear that I might say or do the wrong thing, or that I might disappoint Grandmère in some way.

I had no idea what official duties my grandmother was expected to perform. All I really knew was that we would visit Aunt Anna and her husband, Jim Halsted, who were living in Shiraz, Iran. Jim was a Fulbright Scholar in internal medicine, who was studying intestinal diseases and working with Iranian physicians as they established the new Namazi Hospital, associated with the Pahlavi University Medical School in Shiraz. Later I learned that part of the trip was for my grandmother to report her impressions of how American foreign aid to Iran was being utilized so that the U.S. delegation to the United Nations could be better informed about progress under the Shah. While in Israel my grandmother had scheduled several speaking engagements and was on a fact-finding tour to understand what progress had been made with the settlement of Jewish refugees, as well as how Israel was dealing with the nomadic Arab tribes that continued to roam the desert, ignoring state boundaries, as they had for centuries.

Grandmère's visit was timed to coincide with the opening of the Eleanor Roosevelt Youth Aliyah school in Israel. Youth Aliyah was originally established in 1933 to help get Jewish youths out of Nazi Germany and into Palestine. After the war its mission evolved to meet the needs of orphaned refugee children from all over the world so that they could settle in their new country, get an education, and have their health and social needs met. In the late 1950s, Israel's statehood, having been established in 1948, was still not recognized by most Arab states. My grandmother continued to be involved with discussions to ease tensions between Israel and her neighbors—Lebanon, Egypt, Syria, Jordan, and what was at the time Palestine, now the disputed territories of the West Bank and Gaza.

Before we went on our trip, Grandmère gave me a copy of Leon Uris's novel *Exodus* to read. I was surprised that she had given me a novel rather than a history book about Israel. The issues surrounding Israel's statehood were so fraught with a complicated history and entrenched emotion that Grandmère wanted me to get a sense of the passions held by those who had fought for the establishment of the state that was their ancestral homeland, as well as an understanding of the sense of loss experienced by those who fought to remain on the land they also claimed as their homeland. Reading *Exodus* did give me an introduction to the long-held ideals and willingness to fight for and defend a homeland. In addition, the names of cities, towns, and sacred shrines became more familiar, so that I had a better sense of what I would be seeing as we drove around the country.

When spring of 1959 and the time for our trip arrived, Grandmère gave me a copy of our itinerary that only included some of the main stops. Without the expectation that there would be people to help carry our luggage, I carefully packed everything I would need in one suitcase. By the end of our trip, I would be so sick of wearing the same clothes again and again that I never wanted to see those few outfits again.

On March 11, 1959, Grandmère and I boarded a TWA Jetstream propeller plane, also known as the Lockheed L-1649 Starliner, bound for Paris, our first of four stops on the long journey to Shiraz, Iran.

Jet airplanes did fly to Europe in 1959, but I remember Grandmère saying they were too new to trust, especially since she had her granddaughter along on the trip. As soon as we got on the plane bound for Paris, Grandmère buckled her seat belt, pulled out some papers from her briefcase, put them on her lap, nodded her head, and promptly fell asleep. This, I learned, was how my grandmother traveled—she slept most of the way. I was far too excited to even think about sleeping. I kept my nose against the window looking at the disappearing ground until finally there was only darkness below. We left in the late afternoon from New York and flew through the night, stopping to refuel in

Figure 6.1. Leaving for Europe and the Middle East. *Source*: Trans World Airlines, courtesy of ZUMA Press.

Goose Bay, Labrador, in northeastern Canada, before landing on a chilly, rainy morning in Paris where we were to change planes and continue on to Rome.

When we boarded the next plane for Rome, Grandmère went through her routine and fell sound asleep for the next few hours until we landed. In Rome we did check into a hotel, but Grandmère had arranged for a friend of hers to show us around the city. Grandmère's March 1959 "My Day" column described her friend, "Countess Lea Lelli, the most interesting guide one can have. She describes the history of Rome as though she had lived through each century, and had experienced each conquest, and I can think of no one who could have given us a more interesting bird's-eye view of the cities as they grew up on the different hills, for the afternoon and evening we would be there." Countess Anna Lea Lelli was descended from a Roman family closely aligned, for four hundred years, with the Vatican. Grandmère said I could have a few minutes to freshen up before we would meet our Roman guide for lunch. By this time, I had not slept for at least twenty-four hours and could have easily fallen asleep. Sleep, however, was not an option. The noisy Roman streets certainly woke me up, and the whirlwind tour of this majestic city, visiting all seven hills, kept my head buzzing with historical dates and facts, architectural information, and the stories of Roman life with which our guide regaled us. Even though Grandmère had arranged for this guided tour because I had never been to Rome, she was fully engaged, asking questions about architecture, history, and how Rome's ancient heritage was incorporated into modern Roman life. Rome, we were told, must be seen at night as well as during the day, so after dinner we three marched off again to see the Spanish Steps, the Coliseum, and the Vatican all lit up. Looking back on my introduction to Rome, I am grateful that I was able to be in so many places I had read about and was actually able to feel a part of this ancient city, which I would visit again. It was late by the time we returned to the hotel. Grandmère and I agreed to meet at 7:00 the next morning for breakfast in order to get to the airport for our next flight to Ankara, Turkey.

Exhausted by our whirlwind tour of Rome, and a with mere three or four hours of sleep, I marveled that my grandmother, at breakfast, seemed full of energy. The sun was just breaking through the clouds as we left for the airport to board the plane flying to Ankara. Grandmère did a bit of reading this time, but it wasn't long before her head hit her chest, and she was sound asleep. Although our time in Ankara was only a few hours, we were provided with an extraordinary tour of the culinary flavors of Turkey. Local government officials and people Grandmère had met during her time in the UN arranged for a feast to honor her. Our plates, a kaleidoscope of color and taste, were piled high with yellow saffron rice, deep green stuffed grape leaves, yellow and green lentils, meats covered in red and brown sauces, vegetables of every color, and multiple varieties of olives in colors from black to all hues of green—it was more food than I could possibly eat. My mother had warned me never to eat anything that had not been cooked for fear of getting diarrhea. I must admit I chose not to listen to my mother's warning, which I felt would be rude in the face of this incredible array of foods. By the time dessert was being served, we were already saying our good-byes and rushing back to the airport for our next flight, which would take us to Iran and my relatives.

As soon as we found our seats on the flight to Iran, reverting to form, Grandmère sat down, adjusted her seat belt, let her chin fall to her collar bone, and fell sound asleep. I now realized that much of her extraordinary energy came from her ability to fall asleep immediately in most any setting. Grandmère had spent an extraordinary amount of time traveling all over the world—as First Lady and later as U.S. delegate to the UN, or on fact-finding tours for the U.S. government. And she was constantly asked to speak to nongovernmental organizations representing an array of social issues. Many of her travels were intended simply to bring back whatever she learned from talking with ordinary people about conditions of life in other countries. In her role as private citizen, she continued traveling on behalf of nongovernmental and private organizations promoting health, education, civil rights, and democratic ideals. Not one to want to waste time when she could be meeting with people or touring a given area, Grandmère learned to sleep when and wherever there was a lull in activity. As our trip progressed, I found this to be true under any circumstances. I tried to follow her example, but as on our transatlantic flight, I found myself too excited to sleep. I found this time useful for making notes in my diary so that I would not forget all these new sights, smells, and sounds.

As the constant drone of the plane's engines drew us east-ward toward a line of bright pink in the sky, the black night and the stars' brilliance faded slowly, pushed to the other side of the globe. Fingers of the sun began waking the desert. Suddenly the city of Tehran appeared below us. Dazed in the bright, early morning light, Grandmère and I stepped from our plane and walked toward the customs and immigration office, where we presented our passports to the official greeting us, and with a cursory glance and a nod, our passports were quickly returned. I wanted to have a large official stamp of the country as a memento on my passport, but somehow I knew this was not the time to ask why we were not being treated as we had been when going through all the other customs stations. Typically, Iran and Israel both forbade travelers with a country stamp from the other country from entering their country. Grandmère later explained that she had made special arrangements with the governments of Iran and Israel to be allowed to travel from one country to the other without a stamp. Travel restrictions were a continuing source of friction throughout the Middle East and continue to be so today.

Without a moment's hesitation, we returned to the tarmac where a small, twin-engine prop plane waited to take us to Shiraz, a city south of Tehran. This plane was normally used for transporting cargo between Tehran and smaller cities around Iran and did not have customary airplane seating. Instead, there were two metal benches along each side of the fuselage with seat belts indicating where we were supposed to sit. Without cushions, the chill of our seating arrangement soon crept through my clothes. It felt as though we were sitting on a block of ice. Other than the pilot, Grandmère and I were the only people on the plane. Such discomfort fortunately eluded Grandmère, who once again fell sound asleep. She had traveled in small planes like this many times, but for me it was quite an adventure. The plane took off, climbing toward the snow-capped Elburz Mountains near Tehran, and soon banked over the vast dunes heading south. We flew low enough that I could clearly see the pristine desert below. With the gradual shifting of the sun, the sand turned from a grayish brown to a deep gold on the way to becoming a white glare. The barren and gently sculpted dunes seemed to go on forever. Dark shadows cast on the desert floor before the sun reached its zenith made the desert resemble an undulating black and gold painting.

I spotted one small line of five camels carrying bundles with a robed figure riding the lead animal. With each step it appeared as if the camels sank into the loose sand. From the air, this up-and-down motion emphasized the slow rhythm of desert travel. As our plane neared Shiraz, palm trees suddenly appeared clustered around small square buildings glistening in the early morning light. Grandmère bolted awake as our plane bumped along the short airstrip, punctuating the end of our journey halfway around the world.

Aunt Anna and her husband, Jim Halsted, greeted us warmly and regaled us with stories of this small desert city.

They lived in a simple, comfortable, stucco house in a quiet neighborhood of similar houses. Walking up to their home, I noticed a strong odor in the air and quickly dismissed it as car fumes even though I saw few cars in the streets. Later I realized that no matter where I went in Iran the air smelled the same— Iran's air, like their politics, was soaked with oil.

When Anna asked me if I wanted anything to eat, I had no idea if I was hungry for breakfast, lunch, dinner, or even hungry

Figure 6.2. Arrival in Shiraz, Iran. *Source*: Personal collection of the author.

at all. My sense of time was completely disrupted. Grandmère, on the other hand, was full of energy and ready to start sightseeing. We did, however, relax over a simple lunch of fresh fruits and a green salad prepared and served by Anna and Jim's house servant. Anna explained that her Iranian employee considered it an affront to his professionalism if she did any work around the house. When Anna had once begun to weed her own garden, he had been horrified, waving his arms and exclaiming, "What is the matter? You must not do this!" Anna, in typical Roosevelt fashion, respected the houseman's cultural norms but busied herself around the garden and house when he was not there. This knowledge marked my introduction to the role of women in cultures other than my own. In Iran, Anna was considered a woman of an elite class who never did any sort of physical work and was pampered by servants. Regardless of their social class, however, women were of little consequence, having no purpose other than to produce male children and serve their husbands and other male family members.

On our first day in Shiraz, Jim took us on a tour of the Namazi Hospital. Jim knew that my grandmother would want to see everything, including the kitchens, the food being served, and all the support areas for patients of differing ages. We started in the kitchen, peered into the steaming pots of rice and what looked like a stew, examined the pantry to see what sort of supplies were kept, and even looked at special dietary menus. We went to the operating room, examination rooms, and finally the patient wards. Grandmère's primary concern was the well-being of the patients. She never hesitated to ask probing questions. Grandmère wanted to know how often the rooms were cleaned, what the ratio of nursing staff to patients was, and how medical information was communicated to the patients. Additionally, she asked about the patients' living conditions, how far they had to come to receive medical help, and of course, she wanted to know about their children's health and education.

The Namazi Hospital looked like a normal hospital with one exception. During our tour we noticed at the back of the hospital were open courtyards with pens filled with sheep, goats, and chickens. These were not for patient food but rather the private farm animals of the patients. A male patient, surrounded by several family members, explained to Grandmère that, in order for him to come to the hospital, he had to bring his animals for fear they would be stolen while he was away. This was typical of many patients who, due to the distance traveled, had to bring their families and livestock to the hospital for fear of what might happen if they were left unattended. Family members could be seen sleeping on the floor or in crude shelters erected to protect them from the elements. While Grandmère was pleased that people had a place where they could seek medical attention, she was concerned that medical care was not more accessible and closer to where the villagers lived. She knew that often unusual accommodations were necessary—it was my grandmother's gracious way of accepting and respecting cultural differences that has influenced me throughout my life.

We visited a child whose bed was surrounded by many family members wringing their hands, eyes darting back and forth between the child and the rest of the ward, clearly worried. Their anxiety was not only for their child, but due to the hospital noises, smells, and general hustle and bustle so unfamiliar and disconcerting for this rural, desert family. The boy's father explained that their son had to have "some bad thing taken from his stomach," but the doctors were going "to save the life of their eldest son." Uncle Jim smiled and added, "The boy had an appendectomy."

During a later conversation, in addition to explaining the practice of animals joining the patients at the hospital, Uncle Jim told us he'd been dismayed to learn that women did not have a role in their own medical care. Women were never included in decisions concerning their own health, nor with the care of their children. As a physician, Jim was not allowed to examine a female patient, of any age, unless the male head of the family gave his permission. Male family members insisted on being present during such examinations as well as during procedures performed on the women. Vaginal examinations were typically denied by the family patriarch. Grandmère understood this to be the case in many countries. She mentioned that there were programs to encourage more women to go into medicine, but that was also difficult since women were rarely granted the necessary access to education that men were routinely granted in most of these same countries.

Leaving the hospital, Anna drove us through the streets of Shiraz. We noticed an elaborate system of ditches with flowing water. Anna explained that for many people in the city the only available water ran through these ditches along the side of the streets. The city was divided into sections with a series of gates controlling the water flow. One by one, for short periods of time, water was brought to each neighborhood. Depending on the supply, water was not always available on a daily basis. Grandmère and I watched as children splashed in the same water where women did their laundry, washed dishes, and bathed themselves and their children. Slightly separated from the women, men came to the edge of the ditch to bathe, and it was not uncommon to see the water as it wound its way through the city being used as a toilet. The water system had been engineered so that the cleanest water entered the wealthy district first. As the water flowed through successive neighborhoods, reaching the poorest last, it became more and more polluted. It was dangerously polluted by the time it reached the poorest people In Shiraz. Shaking her head, Grandmère sighed, "This is one reason there are so many problems with disease in Iran."

Grandmère had asked to see how the rug merchants lived and worked. Anna arranged for us to visit several rug weavers in an area of Shiraz. On a narrow cobblestone street fit only for donkey carts, in small, square, poorly built huts, weavers moved their fingers with lightning speed as they practiced their ancient art. While Grandmère stopped to talk with several of the men, groups of children raced through the street to gawk at the strange foreigners. One toothless man, whose lined face made him appear older than he was, invited us into his shack, which served both as his workshop and his home. In the corner of the single room, hidden by thin curtains, was an area for storing cooking pots, clothing, and other household items. The well-swept dirt floor of the remaining part of the room had a low, worn, wooden plank table with several cushions scattered around and, in the corner, several tightly rolled carpets that were used as sleeping mats. The only natural light in their home came from the doorway. There was an oil lamp in the corner. Our host barked an order in Farsi to his wife, then politely continued showing us how he made his carpets. His wife and three daughters emerged from behind the curtain and offered us thick, sweet coffee and chewy fruit-tasting candy. Even though we had not expected any refreshments, we also knew it would be an insult to refuse. My grandmother was offered the largest cushion to sit on. Awkwardly, yet with amazing grace, Grandmère lowered herself onto the cushioned floor. As soon as we were settled, the matron and her daughters retreated behind the curtain; only the males of the family remained to enjoy the treats.

We had noticed rugs laid out on the streets, and Grandmère asked our host, "Why are the newly woven rugs put in the middle of the roadway to be trampled?"

Through our interpreter, the weaver explained, "Mrs. Roosevelt, we do this to make the carpets look old because Americans like antique carpets."

Grandmère also asked our host about his family. She wanted to know: Were his children learning to weave? Did they go to school? Had they been immunized against childhood diseases? This line of questioning, now familiar to me, reflected Grandmère's concerns about every aspect of ordinary people's lives, especially how children were treated. It was the man who answered her questions. Grandmère knew the children's mother was a few feet away behind the thin curtain but would never be allowed to answer these questions. Women were expected to remain silent unless the husband allowed her to speak. As we were leaving, the wife and daughters reemerged to say good-bye. My grandmother grasped the wife's hand and thanked her for her hospitality and complimented her on the health of her children.

While most of the time in Shiraz was spent understanding how people lived in this part of the world, we did visit several incredible mosques. At the Vakil Mosque, built between 1751 and 1773 by the Zand Dynasty, we took our shoes off before entering and were in awe of the dramatic space before us. Light filtering in from all directions brought to life the colors of the forest of columns, arches, and intricate tile work. At one time the area surrounding this mosque was a busy trading and arts center. The tiles throughout the mosque are examples of tiles made in Shiraz. The Nasir al-Mulk Mosque was equally awe-inspiring and famous for its Orsi stained glass.

Figure 6.3. A mosque in Shiraz. *Source*: Personal collection of the author.

Figure 6.4. A mosque for theological studies in Shiraz. *Source*: Personal collection of the author.

On a warm, sunny day we drove with Anna, Jim, and an interpreter to the ancient city of Persepolis, where we planned to picnic. On our way Grandmère had planned a stop at a large farming operation that had been given tractors by the United States to increase food production for the area. When we arrived, about twelve men stood in front of a long line of shiny new tractors. Obviously, the tractors had not been used for any sort of plowing. When asked why the tractors had not be used, our host, who appeared to be a supervisor, kept saying in broken English, "Yes, we use, not many know to drive." By the time we got back in the car, my grandmother was shaking her head and said she was surprised that more workers had not been trained to drive the tractors and that they were going to waste. Jim commented that, without the Iranian government intervening, the tractors would soon be sold or taken apart. Clearly, Grandmère was dismayed.

Continuing on toward Persepolis, along the roadside, in front of a small, rounded, white-washed mud hut, a thin, elderly, bearded man sat with legs crossed as if in deep meditation. At the sound of our approaching car, he stretched his arms forward with palms turned toward the sky.

"Jim, please stop, I'd like to talk with this man," Grandmère said.

As Jim slowed the car, our interpreter explained that this was a blind beggar who had been here for many years. He lived off the kindness of passersby. Grandmère, with our interpreter at her side, began to greet the man but was suddenly interrupted by this blind man, who raised his arms to the sky and with great clarity exclaimed, "Mrs. Eleanor Roosevelt!"

The mere sound of my grandmother's voice was so recognizable that it brought a broad smile across his weathered, wrinkled face. When Grandmère tried to talk with the man, all he could do was repeat, "Mrs. Eleanor Roosevelt, Mrs. Eleanor Roosevelt, you've come to see me . . ." He reverently held the hem of her skirt and bowed, tears glistening in the sunlight as they fell from his opaque eyes. Without any visible means of communication, this man must have heard my grandmother's voice at one time and now, in isolation in the desert of Iran, knew who my grandmother was, what she represented, and revered her. We left our picnic food with him and drove toward the ruins of Persepolis.

The sixty-foot-high columns of this once-great city loomed against the intense blue sky. Persepolis had been built during the reign of Darius I, beginning in about 515 BCE at the apex of the Persian Empire. Designated as the seat of government, it was mostly used during the spring and summer. Stones, cut with precision from the nearby mountain, were laid without mortar to create the grand buildings that made up this city, representing the wonders of the Persian civilization. Alexander the Great, who came to plunder Persepolis in 330 BCE, used nearly three thousand camels to carry all the treasures away. I was in awe of this sacred, historic place as we climbed through the ruins of Darius

Figure 6.5. Persepolis. *Source*: Personal collection of the author.

Figure 6.6. Persepolis. *Source*: Personal collection of the author.

I's and Xerxes's palaces, admiring the stunning carvings and the stone work that remains.

Leaving the ancient glory of the Persian Empire and Shiraz, Grandmère, Anna, and I accepted the formal invitation of the American ambassador, Sheldon Chapin, to stay at the embassy compound in Iran's modern capital, Tehran. Because this was a formal visit, itineraries for each of us were provided. Grandmère, accompanied by Anna, spoke at diplomatic gatherings, while I was treated to a whirlwind of social activities with people my own age.

One of the only events we attended together was lunch at the Golestan Palace with Mohammad Reza Shah Pahlavi. It was in this compound of mosaic-tiled buildings, used at this time for ceremonies and visits from dignitaries, that the famed Peacock Throne was housed. Our luncheon, held in one of the palace's ornate dining rooms, had a long, wide table set with glittering silverware for the five-course meal. The Shah sat on one side of the table with my grandmother opposite. High-ranking Iranian ministers filled the rest of the chairs with Anna and me farther down the table. My grandmother, aunt, and I were the only women scattered among the male-dominated Iranian government officials. Most attended the luncheon in military uniform heavy with medals and ribbons, while others wore dark business suits. My grandmother used this opportunity to speak with the Shah about all of her concerns for the people of Iran and how the U.S. might effectively provide aid. I remember my grandmother speaking about the unused tractors we had seen. She told the Shah that if the Iranian government could not train their farmers to use the equipment donated from other countries, more people would remain near starvation. It was the government's responsibility to utilize the aid received from foreign governments. Then, without stopping, she went on to talk about the necessity for clean drinking water throughout Iran. It was clear to me that the Shah did not really want to listen to what my grandmother had to say, as he often deflected her inquiries about health care, agriculture, and educational progress to others while he looked away, uninterested.

The Iranians were clearly relieved when our luncheon was over. As we rode back to the embassy, Grandmère later remarked, "With so much aid from the United States, one would think they would have begun modernizing their agricultural practices." I could tell by the sharpness in Grandmère's voice that she was not pleased with Iran's lack of progress nor with the Shah's leadership.

Looking back on these interactions, I realize how well prepared my grandmother was when she met with leaders. She had visited the people in need, she had gone to the fields, talked with farmers, visited schools and hospitals, and had all the statistical information our government provided to the public. My grandmother's belief in facing problems with facts and offering solutions no doubt intimidated leaders like the Shah of Iran.

On our last evening in Tehran, I attended a dinner party for "young people" hosted by an American couple living in Iran. Being very shy I dreaded the evening, but when I arrived I found everyone to be friendly and in a particularly festive mood. I soon learned that this evening marked the Iranian New Year, which was treated gleefully with dinner parties and dances across the city. After the dinner party, held at an American diplomat's house and attended by the adult children of Iranian business and government officials, I was escorted by a young man from a well-respected Iranian family to a private club. Upon entering the club's palatial entryway, I noticed, hanging from the high ceiling, an elegant, multitiered chandelier, each crystal like a cluster of stars. Music and laughter came from several rooms at the top of a long, red-carpeted stairway leading to a balcony overlooking the central hallway. The women wore beautiful modern dresses adorned with splendid jewelry—not a chador (a traditional full-body wrap that covers the head but exposes the face) in sight. It was truly a glittering party complete with all sorts of food, drink, dancing, and singing, which continued throughout the night. It was early in the morning before I climbed the embassy's elegant staircase to my bedroom. As soon as I opened the door, I noticed a note from my grandmother lying on my pillow:

Nina Dear,

Anna says you mind waking me, but I feel happier to know you are safely home & I go right to sleep again. So do come in & say goodnight.

Love, Grandmère.

Afraid that she would look at her clock and see that I had been out very late, I turned the clock to face the wall and gently kissed Grandmère on her cheek. I had hoped to sneak out quickly. However, Grandmère immediately awoke and said, "Yes, Nina, you do look as lovely as Anna said." Turning the clock back around, she kissed me and said good night.

After a short sleep, still wishing for more, we left the embassy and went to the Tehran airport for our flight to Israel. Once again, our passports were looked at, but no stamp of embarkation was given. Similarly, when we arrived in Israel our passports were looked at and then given back with no stamp indicating that we had ever entered the country.

CHAPTER 7

Israel

The muted sounds of an awakening city warming itself in the soft orange light of dawn could be heard through the open windows in the dining room of Jerusalem's King David Hotel. Ringing bells, chanting, and prayers—instead of the usual cacophony created by big city traffic—filled the streets on this Easter Sunday morning in 1959. As Grandmère and I ate breakfast in the dining-room, a steady breeze pushed the filmy, white organza curtains out of the way to welcome us as the first guests of the morning. Grandmère ordered her usual toast with bacon and hot water with a dash of tea and milk. I had cold cereal and toast with local honey.

The King David Hotel was built of large rectangular stones that, like desert sands, changed colors as the sunlight inched its way across their uneven surfaces. At dawn they looked pale orange, later in the day reddish yellow, and changed to gold with pink flecks as the day progressed and the sun sank lower. By evening the last rays cast a blue hue over these stones carved from ancient earth.

Because finding a taxi or taking public transportation would be difficult on this holy day in this most holy of cities, Grandmère had arranged for a car and driver to take us to the Church of the Holy Sepulcher. The streets of Jerusalem, under a cloudless sky, were empty of vehicular traffic, with most people observing their religious rituals in this holy site for Muslims, Christians, and Jews. As our car wound through the narrow, cobblestone streets toward the Christian Quarter on Golgotha Hill in one of the oldest parts of the city, we passed lines of clerical men and women dressed in black robes, their heads bowed, rosaries running through their fingers. Since Jordan had evicted all Jewish people from what is known as the "Old City" in 1948, Jewish worshippers were still barred from entering this area, which contained many sacred Jewish buildings. Observant Jews, dressed in black, with yarmulkes perched on their heads, and holding prayer books, ambled along the sun-drenched streets of the "newer" but still ancient parts of Jerusalem with lowered heads. Laypeople from all over the world reverently walked the paths, headed in no particular direction except to breathe in every inch of the city that bore witness to some of the most holy, and most violent, days in the history of organized religion.

Our driver let us off at what looked like the opening of a cave. Anticipating my question, Grandmère, who had visited Israel many times, turned to me and whispered, "Nina, parts of this church date from the time of the Crusades." With a smile and a twinkle in her eye, she added, "People were much shorter then, as you will see. Be careful not to hit your head." Grandmère and I both were nearly six feet tall, and we learned how to bow our heads, partially in reverence but more practically to keep from banging our foreheads against the stone lintels. As we moved into this holy shrine and found ourselves immediately engulfed in darkness and the lingering smells from hundreds of years of burning incense and candles, I was aware of how small the building really was. The walls, built of irregularly shaped, rounded, and smoothed stones, were damp. With no windows and little circulation, the cool black air felt as though it contained the exhaled breath of an ancient time. We were each handed a long white candle to guide our way. The candles cast only a meager light extending about two inches in front of us. Our Greek Orthodox host, covered in long robes, gestured for us to follow along a path of uneven stones pounded into soft roundness by centuries of the world's footsteps. We proceeded down a short, narrow hall, under low arches to what I believe was a small chapel. On the way, as I followed Grandmère, she looked back at me. Without speaking, she nodded her head in the direction of a stone. I knew this must be the Stone of Unction where Jesus's body had been anointed. In a few more steps we entered a small, cave-like room. Our candles revealed years of black residue that had built up on the stone walls, which gave the room a somewhat sinister appearance.

Grandmère had explained that we would be attending a Greek Orthodox service in the Chapel of St. Helena, named for the Emperor Constantine's mother, who reportedly found the cross of Jesus in this place. The small chapel was filled with worshippers who may also have been tourists. Grandmère and I were directed to the front row of four rows of narrow, wooden, straight ladder-backed chairs. A couple of feet in front of us, stood an imposing priest dressed in long white robes. His vestment consisted of a shawl of gold and green embroidered symbols that hung from his neck to the floor. A tall pointed hat securely affixed to his head was decorated with threads of gold, and his long white beard nearly matched the color of his robe. Behind the high priest stood a bank of tall, fat, long-burning candles surrounded by smaller ones. Their light swayed back and forth in unison with the air seeping in from invisible cracks in the wall and the bodies settling into chairs to be led, step by step, through the ancient ritual. Two young boys hidden in the background rushed forth on cue to hold a massive book and a golden chalice. This highly ritualized ceremony reenacted the story of the angels who rolled the stone away from the door of Jesus's grave and had told the women waiting beside the tomb, "Go quickly, and tell His disciples that He is risen from the dead . . ."

Carefully cradling our candles with both hands, Grandmère and I took our seats. By this time our candles were dripping wax on to the paper wrapped around them. The paper served only to cool the wax before it reached our hands. I watched to see how Grandmère was holding her candle, hoping to discover a way to keep my hands from becoming waxy globs by the end of the service. Grandmère had carefully placed a white handkerchief bordered by dainty lace over her hands. Her small action made it all look even more reverent, but it was a purely protective measure. As soon as we sat down, Grandmère wiggled back and forth to adjust her bottom on our very uncomfortable chairs, settling in like a chicken on her nest. Within seconds of being seated, I glanced again at Grandmère. Her head was bowed, her chin was resting near her collarbone, and she was seemingly engrossed in prayer. Actually, my grandmother was sound asleep thanks to her wonderfully useful capacity to nod off at a moment's notice whenever she sat down. However, I was quite anxious. Fearing that Grandmère might set herself on fire if the candle slipped, I nudged her foot with mine to wake her. No response. Then I nudged her harder, and still no response. Now terrified that she would loosen her grip on the candle, I decided to try to push her arm just enough to awaken her. That did the trick. Grandmère moved slightly, looked over at me, smiled, tightened her grip on the candle, and went right back to sleep. Upon leaving the Church of the Holy Sepulcher, refreshed from her nap, Grandmère walked with the agility of a young woman along the uneven cobblestone street. As we walked, Grandmère pointed out other historical spots along the Via Dolorosa.

One of the reasons Grandmère had been invited to Israel was to participate in the twenty-fifth anniversary celebrations of Youth Aliyah. A worldwide organization, Youth Aliyah had been instrumental in bringing orphaned refugee children of Jewish heritage to settlements in Israel and training them for leadership positions in their ancestors' homeland. Grandmère's efforts on behalf of refugees fleeing war-ravaged Europe after World War II had contributed significantly to the settlement of hundreds of children and families, particularly in Israel. Due to these and other efforts, Grandmère was the only non-Jewish woman to have a Youth Aliyah center named after her. The Eleanor Roosevelt Youth Aliyah settlement in Beersheba was dedicated in March 1959.

Prior to the dedication ceremony, Grandmère and I toured the facility with many of the children and staff. The children,

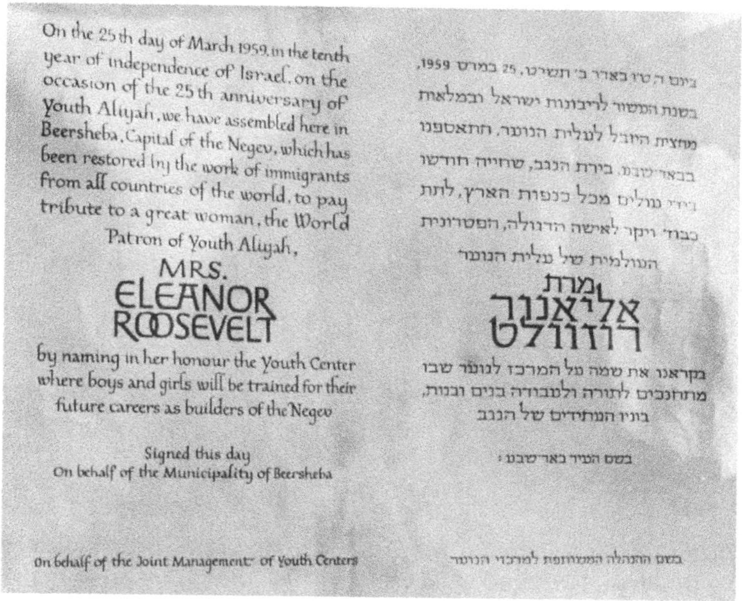

On the 25th day of March 1959, in the tenth year of independence of Israel, on the occasion of the 25th anniversary of Youth Aliyah, we have assembled here in Beersheba, Capital of the Negev, which has been restored by the work of immigrants from all countries of the world, to pay tribute to a great woman, the World Patron of Youth Aliyah,

MRS.
ELEANOR
ROOSEVELT

by naming in her honour the Youth Center where boys and girls will be trained for their future careers as builders of the Negev

Signed this day
On behalf of the Municipality of Beersheba

On behalf of the Joint Management of Youth Centers

ביום ה' ט"ו באדר ב' תשי"ט, 25 במרס 1959.

בשנת העשור לריבונות ישראל ובמלאת מחצית היובל לעלית הנוער, התאספנו בבאר־שבע, בירת הנגב, שחזייה חזרשו בניה עולים מכל כנפות הארץ, לתת כבוד ויקר לאישה הדגולה, הפטרונית העולמית של עלית הנוער

מרת
אליאנור
רוזוולט

בקראנו את שמה על המרכז לנוער שבו מתחנכים לתורה ולעבודה בנים ובנות, בוני המחדירים של הנגב

בשם עיר באר־שבע :

בשם ההנהלה המשותפת למרכזי הנוער

Figure 7.1. The Eleanor Roosevelt Youth Aliyah settlement in Beersheba. *Source*: Youth Aliyah, Israel, public domain.

refugees from other parts of the world who spoke many different languages, greeted Grandmère with long-stemmed calla lilies and broad smiles. As they showed us around the property, leading us into each building—including the kitchens, bathrooms, bedrooms, play areas, living areas, work areas, and school rooms—it was clear that the children enjoyed showing off their new home. While we walked, the children, all talking at once, tapped Grandmère's arm or tugged on her coat and with excitement said, "Oh, Mrs. Roosevelt, look at this, it's my painting," or "I planted this."

Thinking back on this experience, I am reminded of a woman I met many years later. She told me a story that could be the story of any one of these Youth Aliyah children. Orphaned as a very young girl, the woman remembered how lonely she

Figure 7.2. Touring the Youth Aliyah with some of the children. *Source*: Youth Aliyah, Israel, public domain.

felt living in a European orphanage among many other displaced children from war-torn France and Germany. Their caretakers were kind but very busy, and personal attention from an adult was rarely part of the daily routine. In her capacity as First Lady, my grandmother had come to visit the children's home. Wanting a photograph to commemorate the First Lady's visit, the head of the school asked Grandmère if she would have her photograph taken with some of the children. The woman telling me the story remembered Grandmère's broad smile as her long arms gathered several children including the storyteller around her in a warm embrace. For a few precious moments, after the photograph had been taken, Grandmère and the children lingered in their closeness. Now, sixty-five years later, with tears in her eyes, this woman remembered the sensation of that hug. She told me that for an instant she did not feel like an outcast, and the hug from my grandmother had sustained her throughout her life. It was her most cherished childhood memory. She knew, as only children can know, the sincerity of a loving hug from Eleanor Roosevelt.

As Grandmère and I toured the Youth Aliyah campus, Grandmère not only asked the cook what the children ate on a daily basis, she proceeded to look in the refrigerators to verify that the food was fresh. Teachers and counselors were asked what subjects the children liked and how they dealt with language differences. The counselors also had to explain the children's emotional health in answer to Grandmère's probing questions. I was especially interested in one of Grandmère's major concerns, the children's physical health, and listened intently as she directed specific questions to the physicians. Here and almost everywhere we went, Grandmère wanted to know exactly what immunizations the children received and how often they were given regular medical checkups.

After our tour, I was honored to unveil the large sign naming the center the Eleanor Roosevelt Youth Center.

Figure 7.3. Nina unveils the sign naming the center "The Eleanor Roosevelt Youth Center." *Source*: Youth Aliyah, Israel, public domain.

Grandmère spoke to the gathered dignitaries and children about the important contributions these children would make to the development of the emerging state of Israel. When we left the children's settlement, Grandmère was elated. As we settled in our car, she said, "It's gratifying to see those children adapting to a happy life and being given the chance to contribute to their country."

On one of our first days in Israel, Grandmère visited a refugee family she had met on a previous visit. During her first visit, Grandmère observed that the family, having recently arrived in this new land, were having difficulty getting settled. On her second visit, Grandmère greeted the children by name and remembered the specifics of the family's difficulties when they initially arrived in Israel. She remembered that the parents had been in poor health mostly due to inadequate nutrition after years of war in their country of origin. Listening carefully to the parents describe the general health of the family, Grandmère asked what foods they were eating and how they were feeling about their transition from their former Soviet bloc country to Israel. Grandmère asked the parents if the children's immunizations were current and if they had started attending school on a regular basis. Pleased with what she learned, we left this family with hugs and smiles.

Golda Meir and David Ben-Gurion were both friends of Grandmère and both helped found the State of Israel—Ben-Gurion was the first and then current prime minister of Israel (1948–1953 and 1955–1963), and Meir would become the fourth prime minister (1969–1974). Our trip would not have been complete without visits to see them both. One Saturday morning we took a taxi to a meeting with Golda Meir, Grandmère's collaborator for the permanent settlement of refugees. The streets were practically bare, but the few people we did see were on foot, holding small black books, which I assumed were prayer books. As we passed a small group of men, they shouted at us, raised their fists in anger, and even tried to push the slowing taxi off the road. Grandmère just smiled and gracefully asked our driver, "Would you rather have us get out so that you don't have to be driving on the Sabbath?"

He turned around and in broken English responded, "I am Jewish, Mrs. Roosevelt, but I am a Reform Jew. You have done many things for my country and my people. I am happy and proud to drive you anywhere you want to go—Sabbath or no."

Golda Meir looked exactly like her photographs—tall, pear-shaped, with silver gray hair pulled back in a bun at the nape of her neck, and dressed in a dark-colored dress and sensible shoes.

Her English was perfect, and Grandmère later told me that although she was born in Russia, she grew up in Milwaukee. Mrs. Meir had kind eyes, which, like my grandmother's, expressed the experience and compassion that only comes from an extraordinary empathy for the suffering of other human beings. The two women mostly discussed issues relating to the large numbers of people immigrating to Israel from war-torn Europe. Prior to meeting with Golda Meir, we had visited refugee families where Grandmère saw for herself their living conditions and, most importantly, the health and education of the children.

Figure 7.4.At a speaking engagement with Golda Meir. *Source*: Youth Aliyah, Israel, public domain.

On another day we drove to the Sede Boker Kibbutz and visited David Ben-Gurion. During the drive I watched the barren open spaces of the Negev desert. The few outcroppings of rocks and boulders waved and wiggled as the light, distorted by heat, arose from the desert floor. It felt as if my eyes were malfunctioning! The sky, unbroken by any clouds, wasn't really blue but rather a glaring white. Our driver, a sallow-skinned man dressed in wispy white trousers and a loose-fitting, white, open-collared shirt, looked to me as if he were in his pajamas—but I am sure he was cooler than we were.

The Sede Boker Kibbutz had been home to David Ben-Gurion and his wife for many years. The former prime minister was a short man with a broad smile and Einstein-like white hair. He welcomed my grandmother with the warmth and simplicity extended not to dignitaries but to old friends who had participated in many battles together, which the young state of Israel had had to endure in order to establish itself as a viable nation in the Middle East. Grandmère talked with Ben-Gurion about Israeli agriculture and the settlement of refugees. She told him about our visit to a new kibbutz near the Sea of Galilee where, as part of their military service, men and women in their late teens and early twenties were establishing a viable settlement by turning the arid desert into fields producing fruits and vegetables. So far, few fields had been irrigated and the process of digging ditches for an extensive irrigation system was ongoing. A few crops, however, had been planted and enough food was harvested to help sustain the kibbutz members, yet on a much smaller scale than these hardworking, dedicated youth ultimately planned for. Their kibbutz, often showered with bullets from rifles fired from the nearby Jordanian border, developed a rotating system of standing guard over their compatriots to protect them while they worked in the open fields.

Ben-Gurion smiled at my grandmother's report and explained that this was part of life everywhere in Israel. Sede Boker, an older, more established kibbutz, had experienced similar problems during its development. Even now, the prime minister explained,

Figure 7.5. Our visit to a new kibbutz near the Sea of Galilee. Photo by Moshe Pridan, National Photo Collection of Israel, Photography Dept., Government Press Office, public domain.

marauders from neighboring Arabic countries (Lebanon, Jordan, Syria, and Egypt) tried to destroy crops and to disturb the members of the settlement. My grandmother listened with a knowing smile and said, "I just wanted Nina to hear from you the dangers of living so near the borders. She would like to spend next summer on a kibbutz, but I don't think her parents will think it safe."

After a tour of Sede Boker's many communal buildings, living quarters, childcare centers, classrooms, recreation centers, laundry, tool sheds, storage areas, and kitchen gardens, we finally gathered in the dining hall for lunch. Everyone who wasn't working far away in the fields joined us for a simple meal of bread, salad, fruit, and rice served cafeteria style. Grandmère seemed to be particularly relaxed in this informal setting so like her own private life. In the company of these jovial men, women, and children, it was easy to forget the struggles this community endured in their daily lives for so many years.

Back in Tel-Aviv the next morning, while eating our breakfast of toast with honey, bacon, and tea, Grandmère and I looked over our schedule for the day. Our first stop was to be at a camel market near Beersheba. Grandmère explained that the camel market would be attended by many of the nomadic tribesmen who still roamed, without concern for borders, between Israel and the neighboring countries. Like the bazaars in the more populated cities, the camel market would not only include the trading of camels. Goats, sheep, and a variety of goods would also change hands throughout the day.

It was a chilly March morning when we drove into the desert. As the sun rose above the distant mountains, it warmed the almond-colored sand, and we could see the smoke from small fires in the distance. As we got closer to the Beersheba market, a predecessor to our swap meets, we could see numerous bundled-up human figures milling among goats, camels, small bony horses, chickens, and carts full of handwoven fabrics of reds, greens, yellows, and a deep royal burgundy. Geometric-patterned carpets in black, pale beige, and brown, woven from natural sheep's wool, were piled in stacks on the ground. Multipatterned, dyed-wool carpets were rolled into tubes and piled up. A few carpets were laid out on the ground for all, including animals, to walk on. All manner of household goods—pots and pans, small wooden chairs, lamps, lanterns, brooms, worn and broken tables—were stacked so high they nearly tumbled out of the rickety wooden carts that carried them to the market. Scattered throughout the market space, small fires warmed tin coffee pots and the hands of the tribesmen hoping to have the chance to sell their goods as well as to catch up on local gossip. The dry desert air blended the odors of the people, wood- or charcoal-burning fires, brewing coffee, musty animals, and the sweet smell of hay into something I have never forgotten.

The vendors were nomadic tribesmen who wore dark brown camel-hair coats over their tribal robes, and covered their heads with the traditional ghutras held in place by black agals (rope-like circles fitting snugly over the cloth ghutra). Their hands were warmed by fingerless, knitted gloves. Even though the headdresses and ill-kept beards covered most of their faces, sparkling dark eyes darted in every direction, assessing who was there, what was being sold, and what kind of a day it might be for their products. Children tended to the animals, giving them water or hay while the elders sat near fires. No matter their age, the men had the astonishing ability to sit with their feet flat on the ground, heels against the buttocks and chins resting near the top of the knees, which left their arms free to gesture wildly while deep in conversation or rapidly running their ever-present "worry beads" swiftly and deftly, one by one, through calloused fingers. Worry beads appeared as a natural extension of their hands as the string of beads glided gracefully, gently clicking with a rhythm unique to each person.

Because I had grown up around farm animals at Val-Kill, I realized that later in the day this place would be engulfed with strong odors of animals and their waste. But for now, it was early enough that the crisp air still held the sense of spring with only a mild reminder that at 9:00 AM we were moving among many typically smelly animals. Following carefully planned instructions, my grandmother was greeted and escorted off to meet the head tribesmen and the most important town officials while I was left with my grandmother's longtime friend, Abba Schwartz. Abba, an American attorney in his late forties, with a few gray hairs at his temples and a quick, broad smile, had collaborated with Grandmère for years on issues concerning immigration and worldwide refugees. Later, in 1962, Abba became the U.S. assistant secretary of state for security and consular affairs. Abba's career was devoted to ensuring that the United States' immigration laws were inclusive so that those fleeing communism would be able to find a safe haven as quickly as possible in our country. Considering himself an accomplished bargainer, Abba was ready to exercise his skill in this market of nomads for whom bargaining was a way of life. Quite casually Abba remarked, "Nina, this is a camel market, so what do you suppose we should do at a camel market?" I responded with a shrug—I had planned to wander around looking at everything on display.

"Don't you think we should buy a camel to live at Val-Kill?" Abba asked. I laughed out loud, knowing full well that Abba had a wonderful sense of humor and was kidding. But, willing to play the game, Abba and I set off to look at camels, pretending to know something about camels and camel bargaining. Before I knew it, Abba was deep in discussion with three of those round, bundled-up figures with shining dark eyes. There were lots of shaking heads, hands rising and falling in the air, raised voices, then lowered voices, sounds of exasperation, and bodies moving close to each other and then darting apart. I felt as if I were watching a well-choreographed dance between the men. Although others joined to create a circle of discussion, Abba seemed to be holding his own with all of them, gesturing, pointing at me and at the cream-colored baby camel that seemed to be the focus of the discussion. The small camel really wasn't so small but was about my height—five feet, ten inches. Suddenly Abba grabbed me by the arm and we were huddled in conversation. I knew Abba was having fun as his eyes were twinkling, but I still thought that this was just some sort of caper that would end with us walking away.

"Do you like this little white camel? Don't you think she would be fun to have in Hyde Park? She is only two years old and the large dark brown camel is her mother."

"Abba, I think the camel is cute, but my father will have a conniption if I come back with a camel."

Abba turned to the tribesmen to quickly reconvene their discussion, like players on a football field deciding their next play. Suddenly the lead tribesman threw his arms in the air, Abba clapped his hands together, and the camel was mine! I was stunned. The tribesman grabbed me by the hand and started pumping it up and down while showing me a nearly toothless grin.

Later I learned that Abba had told them I dearly wanted a camel on our farm in Hyde Park and that he was my agent. Abba proudly whispered in my ear that he had bargained with the Bedouin tribesman and had gotten the price down to a very reasonable amount. Dita Nazor, an aide from the American Embassy who had witnessed the entire conversation with the tribesmen, interrupted and informed Abba that he had, in fact, been bargaining the price up. It turned out that Abba did not know Arabic and had only a vague idea of what he thought he was saying, using Hebrew words. Having had too much fun to be disappointed, Abba was quite pleased to announce that the baby camel was well worth whatever price he had paid.

Suddenly, it appeared that everyone at the camel market was aware that these people from so far away had paid an exorbitant price for a camel, and curiosity brought more and more people to see what was going on. As the crowd became larger and larger and I was trying to fade into the background, my grandmother appeared, her head cocked and her eyes and face in a familiar quizzical expression. Although I was a little afraid she would be irritated with me for allowing this transaction, I was soon relieved. Hearing the news, Grandmère just smiled and assessed the new addition to our entourage with the critical eye of someone examining a prospective new horse purchase. "What will you name your camel, Nina?" Grandmère asked.

Figure 7.6. At a camel market near Beersheba. *Source*: Photo by Paul Goldman, National Photo Collection of Israel, Photography Dept., Government Press Office, public domain.

"Dutchess," I replied. I had decided to name her after the county where I lived. With a glimmer in her eye and a slight smile, Grandmère asked, "What do you think your father will say?"

"He'll be concerned about the cost of feeding a camel, but I can sell rides to help pay for the hay and feed." Grandmère's smile broadened, and I knew the camel was on her way to Hyde Park. What I didn't know was that this baby camel was about to become the center of an international dispute.

Within a few days an Israeli shipping line and El Al, the Israeli airline, presented me with arrangements for the delivery, including speed, safety, and overall comfort for my camel on such a long journey. In fact, each company was volunteering to ship the camel for free if they could use her for publicity purposes. I was quite sure Dutchess would not mind having her picture taken if it resulted in first-class accommodations.

By the time we left Israel for Paris, plans for Dutchess's trip to America seemed to be settled. However, when the U.S. Departments of State and Agriculture learned of the impending arrival of a camel from the Israeli desert, official cables were sent to Abba, who had returned to Washington, D.C.; my grandmother, who at that point was in Paris with me; and officials of the government of Israel, stating that we could not bring a camel into the U.S. from Israel because Israel was a hoof-and-mouth disease area. Israel, offended, sent reply cables protesting the U.S. government's assessment. The government of Israel insisted that their country did not harbor hoof-and-mouth disease; there was absolutely no reason why a camel could not be shipped directly to the United States. Dutchess's departure was put on hold until the governments could work out their differences. Later, while we were in London, Grandmère received a phone call from an upper-level official at the State Department. I heard my grandmother say, "You will have to discuss that with my granddaughter. Dutchess is her camel." I think the official realized Grandmère would not intervene on behalf of the U.S. government. I never received a phone call.

Meanwhile, the camel story had traveled via the news media, and a well-intentioned, sympathetic man from Canada who read about this baby camel waiting to enter the United States, sent a letter to Abba in Washington to suggest that Dutchess be sent to Canada and then enter the U.S. as part of the "Canadian quota for camels." None of us had any idea what the Canadian quota for camel importation might be, but the State Department quickly replied that even through Canada the camel would need to remain in quarantine for at least six months. When the Agriculture Department refused to agree to a specific duration for quarantine of Dutchess, insisting that they would have to be assured that the camel was not carrying any unwanted diseases from Israel, Israel continued to maintain that they were not a hoof-and-mouth disease area and demanded an apology from the U.S. State Department for raising this concern with other foreign importers.

Without assurances that Dutchess would ever be able to live at Val-Kill, I decided that my camel might be happiest remaining in the desert that was her home. Through the tribesmen, who had been kind enough to care for Dutchess during our many weeks of international arguments, and Dita Nazor, from the American Embassy in Israel, a young man was found who had recently been married and needed transportation to get his goods to market. Happily, but with a twinge of disappointment, I agreed to give Dutchess to the young Bedouin and his wife. I have a photograph of the young man proudly receiving Dutchess and grinning broadly. My grandmother appeared relieved with the solution, quite content without further discussions or questions from the press about the Dutchess affair, when there were many more important refugee issues begging for her attention. Daddy was, no doubt, relieved as well.

Sixty years after the fact, I am still amazed that Abba's impulsive purchase became an international incident. I still have several "camels" that only require occasional dusting and provide fond memories of what might have been.

Later that morning, it became hot. The welcoming smells of early morning fires and the sound of animals munching fresh hay had given way to swatting flies and the odor of dusty farm animals. By the time we left the Beersheba camel market that day to pay a visit to Grandmère's longtime friend Sheikh Suleiman, the desert sand shimmered in the heat. It seemed as if we were not driving on a road but instead over hardened sand. The almond-colored desert met the impossibly blue sky in sharp contrast. The desert looked as if long snakes were resting after a meal as the contours of sand rippled in the light breeze. In the distance, I saw a dark speck in the center of what looked like dancing, colored dots. As we got closer, the wind began to stiffen and a few shadows emerged from the small sand drifts, resembling sloping hills. As the dark speck grew larger, I assumed it must be Sheikh Suleiman's tent. With nothing to compete for attention, this structure in the desert wilderness was a stunning sight. Red, yellow, blue, green, orange, claret, and white flags flew all around the tent in a brilliant, gay display. They snapped as the wind blew them almost like a trumpet announcing that this was an important place, not unlike the way the guards and fences around the White House or Buckingham Palace announce the residence of the head of state. The tent itself was drab olive green but somewhat longer and more spacious looking than some of the single-story buildings I had seen in the newly established towns along the Arab-Israeli borders. Our driver stopped the car, positioning it so that my grandmother would step out onto a plush, spotless, cardinal-red carpet leading across the sand to the front entrance of the tent. Literally, the red carpet treatment—desert style.

My grandmother had met Sheikh Suleiman many years before and was now paying a courtesy call to the man who led one of the largest nomadic tribes still freely moving back and forth between Israel and the surrounding Arab countries. As a member of the United States Delegation to the United Nations in the late 1940s, Grandmère became an influential advocate for the health and welfare of refugees following World War II. Carving the state of Israel out of lands previously held by Arab countries had created a number of difficult ethnic refugee problems for the newly settled Jewish settlers as well as for the displaced Arabs.

The Bedouin tribesmen, whose ancient nomadic lifestyle included wandering from place to place over hundreds of miles of open desert, posed a unique and special problem as they refused to recognize national boundaries. While Grandmère understood the Israeli need for a safe and secure border, she also wanted to help find an agreement that would allow the Bedouins to continue their ancient nomadic life. For the ten years since its establishment, Israel's efforts to get the Sheikh and his tribesmen to establish settlements and respect national borders had failed. Grandmère explained to me that for the older tribesmen the nomadic way of life was all they knew and was part of their cultural tradition.

Figure 7.7. Eleanor Roosevelt with Sheikh Suleiman of the Shuval Bedouin tribe and Lieutenant Colonel Michael Hanegbi in Shuval in February 15, 1952. *Source*: National Photo Collection of Israel, Photography Dept., Government Press Office, public domain.

Because Grandmère had helped the tribesmen establish their right to ignore Arab-Israeli borders, she had earned the admiration of many of the Bedouin tribal leaders. Sheikh Suleiman had spent time with my grandmother negotiating on behalf of his people.

He was shocked to learn that my grandmother, a widowed female, traveled throughout the world without a male escort. Women in his culture would never be allowed to travel by themselves and certainly would never be representing the United Nations. Prior to our visit, Grandmère told me about her interactions during previous meetings with the Sheikh. Apparently, Sheikh Suleiman had presented Grandmère with a pearl-handled pistol, for which she thanked him. Later she gave the pistol to her son, my Uncle James. The next time the Sheikh and my grandmother met, he told her that he was still waiting for her to answer his offer. Grandmère was not sure what the Sheikh was talking about and asked him what offer had she not responded to. He explained to her that in the Bedouin culture, the pistol had been a proposal of marriage. He went on to explain that while he would have her reside with and be a part of his harem, unlike other women in the harem, she would be allowed to travel when necessary, although he would insist that she always have the protection of male escorts. In response, Grandmère quite simply explained to the Sheikh that she was very happy as she was and did not feel in any danger as she traveled. As she retold this story to me, it was clear from her downward cast eyes and flushed cheeks that she had been a bit embarrassed by this proposal, but also amused at the absurdity of her becoming part of a nomadic harem.

On this crystal-clear March day, Grandmère wanted simply to pay our respects to an old friend and to discuss the welfare of the tribe. Dita Nazor and I, to show our reverence for Eleanor Roosevelt to the Bedouins, allowed a respectful distance to open before we followed Grandmère from our car down the long red carpet and into the tent. The entrance flap was ceremoniously held back by a robed Bedouin tribesman. Being tall, Grandmère and I had to duck our heads so as to not hit the top of the doorway. Once through the opening, I stood up in the tent and found myself facing twelve men sitting cross-legged on gaily colored, elegant cushions, each one designed with patterns woven in contrasting colors, accented with gold embroidery and gold tassels hanging from each corner. The men sat around a low, U-shaped, shiny black table arranged with large silver plates, each one overflowing with fruits, pastries, candies, and nuts. Silver coffee urns surrounded by small, round, handleless cups were the focal point of this elaborate display of artistic arrangement and color.

Gazing about I noticed unframed pictures cut out of magazines that were attached to the fabric walls of the tent. To my utter shock, the pictures showed women clad only in lacy underwear or naked, posed in sexually provocative positions. It occurred to me that these lewd depictions might be more appropriate for display in the men's room of a gas station. As my eyes continued to explore all the pictures hung around the tent, I discovered, centered in the back of the tent, two framed pictures—one of Queen Elizabeth and one of Grandmère, both (thankfully) fully clothed. The shock of these revered women appearing with the pin-up photographs made me start to giggle. No sooner had I stiffened up when my grandmother, sensing exactly what was going through my head, turned to me, giving me one of her stern looks that said, *Behave yourself! Do not acknowledge what you are seeing.*

We arranged ourselves on the large cushions opposite the men and were handed cups of the sweet, thick, dark coffee, and a plate of candied pastries and pieces of fruit. Sheikh Suleiman acknowledged my grandmother's visit, inquired about her trip and her comfort on her journey, and proceeded to present us with gifts. I was presented with a blanket made of camel hair and woven in many beautiful colors. The sheikh said through an interpreter, "This is for your camel." How could the Sheikh have known that I had purchased a camel? There was no telephone communication in this part of the desert, and I didn't think they had carrier pigeons. Sheikh Suleiman even knew that I had named the camel Dutchess! Later, when I asked Grandmère how he knew, she explained that the Bedouin were famous for incredible communications and that it was known that one must never think you can keep a secret from a Bedouin. The camel blanket had a split in the middle for the camel's hump and large pockets for whatever cargo I might want to carry. Long, dark-red tassels dangled from all the edges. I could just imagine how it would look against my camel's cream-colored hair flowing gracefully with the swinging movement of camels as they travel across the desert. Today the camel blanket hangs on the wall in my house.

Sheikh Suleiman also presented me with a silver dagger adorned with red and green stones with a hand-hammered pattern along its handle and sheath. Later Grandmère teased me that the dagger must be an offer of marriage to one of the Sheikh's sons, similar to the pistol gift. Although Sheikh Suleiman acknowledged having fifty sons, he had no idea how many daughters he had fathered by the wives in his harem.

When the time came to leave, the Sheikh rose and offered his hand to my grandmother. For a man who refused to acknowledge women as having any worth, standing to say good-bye seemed to me an unusually warm, respectful tribute to this American woman who cared so deeply about the fate of these Bedouin tribesmen. Aware of the unrest between the Arab states and Israel, my grandmother had feared that the Bedouin would lose their way of life, and she became one of the loudest voices in the world community seeking to make their needs known internationally. Peace and stability for the Jewish people resettling in their ancient homeland was of paramount importance to my grandmother, but she also knew that the Arab settlers continued to claim the right to the same territory. Her constant vigilance and negotiating skills were highly valued by both the Jewish and the Arab people.

CHAPTER 8

Paris and London

Grandmère and I flew from Israel as the early morning sun began casting a golden blanket over the rough stones of her historic buildings. I would miss their unique beauty and the way they appeared to change colors between sunrise and sunset as the subtle progression of the sun's rays washed the stones, giving them hues of blue, pink, purple, red, and orange. Flying over the open desert on our way to Paris, we were on our way to a bustling, Western city boasting food, fashion, and art, with a history very different from the Persian, Arab, and Israeli cultures we were leaving. The sky, no longer the intense blue of the arid desert, changed to a dull gray. The brilliant and penetrating Israeli sunshine became a steady drizzle that sparkled on the streets of Paris.

Maureen Corr, Grandmère's secretary, met us at the Crillon Hotel in Paris, a structure with quite a history. Built in 1758 on the Place de la Concorde, the Crillon was the place where Benjamin Franklin and Conrad Alexandre Gérard de Rayneval, the French diplomat, concluded the French-American Treaty recognizing the Declaration of Independence. In 1793 King Louis XVI and his wife, Queen Marie Antoinette, were guillotined in front of what is now this beautiful hotel. Located at the foot of the Champs-Élysées, the hotel afforded us a perfect view of the Arc de Triomphe at the other end of this historic boulevard. The view, when lit up at night, was especially beautiful. While we were in Paris, Grandmère was busy attending meetings, but she made time so we could explore highlights of the city together. Maureen was busy answering telephone calls, typing Grandmère's "My Day" column, and sending off answers to the large stack of mail Maureen had brought with her from New York. No matter where Grandmère might be, she wrote her column, which combined personal notes of what she was doing with observations of the things she saw. Thousands of people looked forward to reading "My Day," which allowed her admirers to feel a part of her life.

We had left one culture and entered another entirely different one. The street noises, architecture, the way people dressed, the food being served in restaurants, and the smells of the city were completely different from the Middle East. I was now in a culture that was more familiar to me. I had studied European history, had been introduced to a smattering of literature and art, and even knew a few words of French. Instead of spending hours walking through museums trying to see as much as possible, my grandmother wisely picked out certain things she felt I would enjoy and allowed time for appreciating those particular pieces. One of the first things Grandmère wanted to share with me was one of her favorite statues at the Louvre, the *Winged Victory of Samothrace*. I remember standing in awe as we viewed the magnificent statue from every possible angle. All these years later, I have in my mind what amounts to a photograph of *Winged Victory* from the first time I saw it.

While Grandmère was busy with meetings, I spent time walking alone along the Seine and window-shopping on the Champs-Élysées, while I kept thinking about the differences between the culture of this city and those of Iran and Israel. My respect for the similarities and contrasts has never left me.

Maureen and Grandmère took me to a restaurant where I was introduced to cheese fondue. With a serious face Grandmère warned me that, when I ate cheese fondue, I should not drink any water or the cheese would form a cold ball in my stomach and cause pain. Maureen nodded her head, and I believed them both. Fondue has a pronounced salty taste and is just the sort of a dish that one wants to drink water with while eating. At first, I did not drink my water, but when I saw others in the restaurant drinking water and eating cheese fondue, I asked again why water was forbidden. Grandmère and Maureen both laughed and admitted that they were playing a joke on me.

A few years before Grandmère brought me to Paris, she had traveled with my brother, Haven, and my cousin, John Boettiger, through Europe. While in Paris, Grandmère thought that college-age boys would enjoy going to Le Lido, the famous nightclub and burlesque show located on the Champs-Élysées. My grandmother referred to the show as entertainment with "scantily clad women." She had made a reservation in order to be assured of a table in this popular club. While she would never have asked for preferential treatment, Haven, John, and Grandmère were ushered to a table directly in front of the stage. Surely, Haven and John were thrilled to be so close, and Grandmère did not seem to mind. A few days later my mother got a letter from my grandmother telling her about their time at Le Lido. Grandmère describes staying "to the bitter end." Haven and John, however, reported that as soon as they sat down and ordered drinks our grandmother fell fast asleep, not waking until the lights came on and the show was over.

Toward the end of our stay in Paris, Grandmère made arrangements for me to experience a little of the French countryside. In between her busy schedule, she took time to arrange for a trip to an old country inn surrounded by grape vines, gardens ready for planting, and blooming fruit trees where we enjoyed a bountiful luncheon. It was a beautiful day, and I enjoyed seeing Grandmère sitting outside with the sun on her face, enjoying the warm afternoon in a moment of peaceful relaxation.

After our usual breakfast, Grandmère, Maureen, and I went to the airport for the short flight to London. There was so much more to see in Paris, I hated to leave after our short, four-day visit. I also knew our magical trip would end soon. Even though my well-worn clothes, which I could not wash myself, needed to be cleaned and my shoes were barely holding together, I was not anxious to go home.

Arriving in London we were surrounded by thousands of stone buildings darkened by soot and huddled together as if to stay warm. London's streets were crammed with red double-decker buses, black taxis, and all manner of traffic darting around parked lorries. Horns honked and the sirens blared in their familiar alternating pitch of Western European emergency vehicles, as people scurried about, heads bowed under black umbrellas, wearing brown or black raincoats, making them look from above like a swarm of bugs.

Grandmère and I were staying at Claridge's, the well-known and elegant hotel in central London. We checked in and were shown to our suite of rooms filled with bowls of fruit and sweet-smelling flowers. I felt like Eloise at the Plaza. Maureen came to London with us to assist Grandmère with her column as well as the correspondence that had piled up while we were in Iran and Israel. On our way from the airport to the hotel we stopped at a side entrance of Buckingham Palace to sign the guest registry. Grandmère explained that as she was a former First Lady of the United States, she was expected to sign the registry for dignitaries from other countries who were visiting London. Later that afternoon, we met at a private club for tea with Lady Clementine Churchill, Winston Churchill's widow. Lady Clementine and Grandmère had become friendly after so many meetings during World War II in England and at the White House. Lady Churchill greeted us warmly, yet formally. As they discussed Grandmère's plans for our stay in London, I learned we were spending the weekend with Lady Stella Reading, a longtime friend of my grandmother's. Lady Reading, who had acceded to her late husband's seat in the House of Lords, was a formidable leader for the resettlement of World War II refugees. Her interest in refugee resettlement, especially of orphaned children, matched that of my grandmother. Both women had spent many years writing and speaking about the health and welfare needs of those who had been displaced to many different countries by the war's devastation. Even though it was fourteen years after the war ended, displaced persons continued to suffer inadequate health care, educational barriers, poor housing, and limited employment opportunities. Lady Reading and Grandmère were vocal advocates for helping families reach and assimilate into their new countries and constantly brought the plight of refugees to the attention of UN ambassadors as well as heads of state. During both world wars, Lady Reading organized the Women's Voluntary Services, which not only assisted the war effort by providing unpaid positions for women but encouraged women to join the workforce in paid employment continuing after the war.

Grandmère and I joined Lady Reading at her London flat for lunch before a planned visit to the House of Lords. Like my grandmother, Lady Reading was tall, large-boned, and dressed in sensible clothes of a classic utilitarian style with comfortable, if not stylish, shoes. The way she walked and spoke left no doubt in my mind that Lady Reading was a forceful, determined woman. As we were finishing our lunch, Lady Reading replaced her napkin in its silver napkin ring, looked at her wristwatch, and informed us, "We will be leaving for the House of Lords in three and a half minutes." Grandmère caught my eye and smiled. When Lady Reading left the room to gather her hat and gloves, Grandmère turned to me and explained, "Lady Reading means it, Nina; she is a very prompt person. We had better be ready to get in the car in exactly three and a half minutes. If you have to go to the bathroom, I'd wait until we get to the House of Lords—you'll have more time there." As predicted, the car and chauffeur stood waiting for us at the front door, and the three of us piled into Lady Reading's car and reached our destination exactly on time.

Lady Reading took her seat on the floor of the House of Lords while Grandmère and I were seated in the visitors' gallery. We both eagerly watched the proceedings from the balcony in this austere chamber. Although I had visited both the United Nations General Assembly and the United States Congress with my grandmother, I had never witnessed what seemed to be common behavior on the floor of the House of Lords. Several members slumped in their large, worn, dark leather chairs emitting loud snores that sounded more like growls. Other lords chatted with each other, paying no attention to the legislative activity. Some members felt it necessary to boo or hiss during the speeches, while others were absorbed in reading newspapers, seemingly unaware of what was being said, making it necessary for others to shout in order to be heard. In general, the lords took this opportunity to act like schoolchildren whose teacher had left the room. To my eyes it truly appeared more like pandemonium than a governing body. "It is often like this, Nina," Grandmère explained. "You would be surprised at the amount of work that actually does get done, but much of it is done prior to entering the floor."

The next day, at exactly 4:29 PM, Grandmère and I stood at the entrance to our hotel with our suitcases packed for a week-end trip to Swansborough, Lady Reading's home in Reading. At precisely 4:30, Lady Reading's car pulled up with Lady Reading at the wheel. We headed for her estate in the idyllic English countryside. Swansborough is a large, sprawling stone manor house with several tall chimneys jutting above the slate roof. The formidable exterior gave no hint of its welcoming, cozy interior. Grandmère and I were shown to our rooms and instructed to "wash up—we'll have supper at 8:00."

The room in which I stayed was dwarfed by a large, antique, four-poster bed covered by a floral-patterned down quilt and several pillows piled against the headboard. A small, lit fireplace was the only source of heat for the room. Next to the fireplace was an overstuffed chair with a standing lamp and a small table covered by a lace doily. On the wall opposite the bed stood an antique chest of drawers, also covered with lace cloth and silver-framed photographs of friends and family. There was room enough for one small table with a lamp and a clock next to the bed. Wall sconces and more family photographs hung on the floral wallpapered walls. I remember the room as a cozy nest. Grandmère's room, although a bit larger, was similar. I don't remember much about the bathroom that adjoined my room except that it had a familiar claw-footed bathtub and chain-pull toilet with a bidet beside it.

During dinner Lady Reading regaled me with stories about her garden and her beloved cats. Later she sent me a book, *Cats in the Belfry* by Doreen Tovey, inscribed, "For Nina, who loves cats. From Stella Reading, Swansborough 1959." I often open this book and remember what a kind force of nature Lady Reading was. After supper Grandmère and I retired to our respective rooms with instructions that breakfast trays would be brought to our rooms at 8:00 AM. I remember climbing into the large bed and sinking into the feathers. It felt as if no part of my body was actually touching anything—I was floating snugly as I drifted off to sleep.

At precisely 8:00 the next morning, a maid knocked softly on my door. "Miss Roosevelt, may I bring your breakfast in?" The room was cold, and I was not certain I wanted to get up at all. The maid brought the tray, and as she was putting it on the bed Grandmère came in wearing her bathrobe and said, "Nina, dear, it is so cold—why don't you come into my room and have breakfast in bed with me?—we'll keep each other warmer that way." Grabbing my robe and my tray, I happily followed Grandmère into her bed, where we arranged the pillows, pulled the down comforter as high as we could, enjoying our moment of snug warmth while we ate boiled eggs and drank hot tea. Mindful of our hostess's precise time schedule, we lingered just long enough to be able to get dressed and be downstairs ready to start our day at the appointed hour.

Lady Reading was a dynamic tour guide. I mostly remember being fascinated by how quickly she could change subjects and the wealth of knowledge she brought to so many topics. Without hesitation she quickly gave me an English history lesson as we passed historic buildings or monuments. While strolling through antique shops, Lady Reading continued the history lesson, describing what the various objects had been used for and who might have owned them. On the road to Stonehenge, we drove by pastures proudly displaying their new green spring color while Lady Reading gave us dairy production figures for the contentedly grazing cattle. Dairy farming and agriculture were sources of income for many of Lady Reading's constituents, and she certainly understood the importance of representing their interests in the government. By the time we reached Stonehenge,

I began to grow weary and longed for the comfort of afternoon tea by the fireplace. However, my two companions, both about four times my age, showed no signs of wear. Both were spry, energetic, and prepared to continue for hours. Fortunately for me, an afternoon drizzle turned to a steady rain, and Lady Reading rushed us through Stonehenge to the car and back to her house before we were drenched. The rain had let up by the time we reached Swansborough, and Lady Reading suggested a tour of her garden before tea. There she carefully identified each flower and described its horticultural attributes. She even advised us which flowers she thought could be grown in Hyde Park and which were best suited for the damp cool English gardens.

It was no wonder Grandmère and Lady Reading were such good friends; they shared many interests, including their concern for the well-being of those in need. I doubted these two women would ever run out of topics to discuss. Their energy seemed boundless.

Back in London, in between Grandmère's speaking engagements, she took me to visit my grandfather's statue in Grosvenor Square and gave me an introductory tour of the British Museum. However, on the afternoon we were invited for tea with Queen Elizabeth, our pace slowed. Since I had little experience with royalty, I asked Grandmère if there were any particular dos and don'ts I needed to be aware of while visiting the Queen of England. Grandmère only cautioned, "Nina, just remember that you never turn your back on the Queen."

We hailed a taxi outside of Claridge's. As Grandmère leaned back in the seat, she said, "Buckingham Palace, please" and instructed the driver to go to the private entrance where friends, family, and those invited for special meetings were received. The cabbie, in a cockney accent sarcastically replied, "And yer goin' ta see the Queen, I s'pose?" As he finished his sentence, he looked in the rearview mirror. Suddenly recognizing his passenger, the cab driver straightened up, touched his hand to his hat in a salute, and trying to correct his native accent, said somewhat timidly, "I guess you are, and I'll take ya there straight 'way, Mrs. Roosevelt."

Grandmère and I exchanged smiles, and we were off for tea at Buckingham Palace.

When we reached the private entrance of the palace, a doorman dressed in a dignified but simple dark uniform with brass buttons opened the door to our taxi and gently steadied Grandmère as she stepped out. Grandmère and I were led down a long, high-ceilinged hall by a lady-in-waiting to large double doors that led into a comfortable drawing room. Heavy draperies hung on the tall windows, which looked out toward a courtyard garden. As expected, the room was palatial. Ornate antique furniture covered in brocade materials and oil paintings of all kinds clearly stated that this was a room enjoyed by many generations of royalty. Despite its formality, the drawing room was comfortable and welcoming. We only had time for a quick glance at our surroundings when a door at the opposite end of the room opened and Queen Elizabeth entered with her hand outstretched to greet my grandmother. The two women greeted each other with smiles and the obvious warmth that comes from shared family experiences. Grandmère presented me to the Queen. Following my grandmother's example and as I had been taught when meeting an elder, I did a slight curtsy, bending one knee and bowing my head with respect. The Queen was very friendly. She immediately told us that two of her children were still suffering from the chicken pox, otherwise she would have included them for tea. Elizabeth guided us toward an intimate grouping of furniture, a couch and two armchairs. Soon a butler appeared from yet another pair of doors leading into a small dining room to announce that tea was ready.

A round table, large enough for four people, was set for three with an ornate silver tea service, silver cutlery, a linen tablecloth, and napkins. Surrounding the arrangement of flowers in the center, there was an assortment of cakes, cookies, sandwiches, toasts, jams, jellies, and honey. Grandmère and I sat on either side of the Queen and watched while she poured tea for each of us. When offered a sampling of all the delicacies I took a piece of toast and some honey and commented that the honey tasted wonderful. The Queen asked me if I liked honey, and I replied that it was one of my favorite things. A knowing smile crossed Elizabeth's face, and she explained that she had honey from all over England and she would like me to try some of the other honeys. She rang for the butler and instructed him to bring in an assortment of honey for this "young honey lover." Other than discussion about honey, my grandmother and Queen Elizabeth discussed the health of the Queen Mother and how difficult it was to get her mother to slow down. Grandmère explained that her children were making similar requests of her. As I munched on the goodies, I listened to the two friends who were obviously enjoying this relaxing visit without the pomp and circumstance of a formal gathering. The Queen did not ignore me, inquiring about my travels and my schooling. Were it not for the appearance of our surroundings, I would have forgotten I was in Buckingham Palace with the Queen of England. Toward the end of our tea, I began to worry about how I would leave the room without turning my back on the Queen. Fortunately, at the close of our visit, the Queen walked with us toward the door and then graciously left the room so that we would not be in the awkward position of having to walk backward out of the room. Mortified that I might trip or fall, I was grateful to the Queen for her thoughtfulness.

As our time in London came to a close, I was returning home filled with memories and experiences that had changed my life. I had seen life lived by nomadic tribes, wandered through ancient streets, visited mosques, cathedrals, and synagogues, listened to the everyday worries of people from cultures different from my own, and experienced sounds, tastes, and smells from a world away. All that I experienced during this trip has continued to form my thinking. What I could never have anticipated was that between the spring of 1959 and the latter part of 1962, a short three years, I would experience losses that taught me very different life lessons.

CHAPTER 9

Sally

At the end of June 1960, I stood at the open screen door, hugged my sister Sally, and told her to have fun riding at Moss Lake Camp. I knew she did not really want to leave Val-Kill, but time was forcing us to grow up. This was the first summer we would all be split up. Haven, who had taken an entry-level summer job with a New York City law firm, assigning himself the important-sounding title of "communications expediter"— otherwise known as "mail boy"—would stay in the city during the week. At seventeen and having graduated from high school a few weeks earlier, with the help of Charles Purcell, I had negotiated a low-paying job at the Hyde Park Playhouse, a summer stock theater run by Gore Vidal, and would remain at Val-Kill. Gore Vidal had been a frequent dinner guest at Val Kill who seemed to enjoy serious political conversations with my grandmother. At the theater, Mr. Vidal was much more relaxed and seemed to enjoy directing the summer productions. Our mother and father preferred to stay in the city during the week. For Mummy the isolation of Val-Kill had finally taken its toll; she never liked country living and resented not having easy access to her friends. Daddy, drained by the two-hour train commute during the summer to Wall Street, looked forward to being free of family and farm responsibilities. It was the summer before the 1960 presidential election, and Grandmère was campaigning across the country for

Adlai Stevenson, who was running for a third straight nomination. (This was before the Democratic Convention in July and at a time when primaries were not determinative.) The Elliott cousins and John Boettiger were also involved with summer jobs or pursuits that dissolved our summer gang. Joanie, too young to go to camp, was being cared for by her nanny, Bea Trombley, in Upstate New York. All of these circumstances made camp seem like a perfect summer solution for Sally at thirteen.

Sally resigned herself to going to the Adirondacks only because she could ride horses nearly every day. Riding was Sally's passion.

"Don't forget to write me—all the time, Nina!" Sally called to me as she walked, half-backward and slowly, down the fieldstone walk toward our station wagon packed with her summer gear. The image of Sally, her thick, shadowy blonde hair pulled back in a ponytail, riding helmet in hand and riding boots carefully laid in their protective cases, tied together at the top and slung over her thin shoulder, remains a vivid picture for me. With each step Sally took that day, my stomach tightened, the air escaped from my lungs, and my heart beat in an uneven syncopated rhythm. Rapidly blinking to stop the tears, I wondered why my sister's going to camp gave me this desperate feeling. Sally and I had been separated many times; I constantly went back and forth between Val-Kill and boarding school and had never been gripped with this kind of feeling before.

We each fell quickly into our new summer patterns and grew used to the separation from each other and from our former lives. Sally wrote and begged us to send cookies and "dims" (dimes) for the Coke machine. I spent most of my time at the summer stock theater, building sets, selling tickets, and once playing a bit part as a "lady of the night" in *The Matchmaker*.

Val-Kill was lonely that summer without the usual number of relatives my age. I even missed Haven bossing us around and my losing at card games to Stewart and Ted Elliott. For the first time, Sally's room remained neat and tidy, but I maintained our normal upstairs clutter by keeping my adjoining room scattered with clothes and books.

I often skipped going home for dinner and joined members of the production staff at MarJoe's, a Hyde Park restaurant, for a quick sandwich before the evening curtain. On the evening of August 12, Cece, the production manager and my boss, had taken me with her for a hamburger and a few minutes of cool air-conditioning at MarJoe's, where we dropped our sweaty bodies into a booth and placed our order. My food had just arrived when I heard the pay phone ringing from its tiny closet-like booth located in a short hall separating the bar from the dining area. Then I heard Joe, the owner, answer with his characteristic slurring, "MarJu's." When Joe came into the dining room, he said, "Nina, it's for you. It's your grandmother." I was surprised and could not understand why Grandmère would call me at MarJoe's.

In the phone booth I pushed my back against the wall and slid onto the triangular seat as I picked up the dangling receiver, "Grandmère?"

"Nina . . . it's Sally . . . you must be very brave. There's been an accident, and I am going to meet Mummy and Daddy at the hospital. I don't know when we will be back. Do you want Les to pick you up?"

Stunned, I was not really certain what she meant. I knew my parents were vacationing in Campobello, and I could not think why I had to be brave. I told her I had to go back to work; the ticket booth was my responsibility that night. Returning to the table, I suddenly felt blinded by the yellow pine of the dining room furniture and avoided looking at any of the familiar faces around the small room. However, I could not shut out the television mounted above my head on the wall shouting news bulletins. There, on the six o'clock news, was a picture of Sally, laughing, her white, slightly crooked front teeth making her grin look more impish than her cocked head. On the screen, her image was immediately haunting and her eyes seemed to be trying to tell me something I never expected to hear. "Sally Roosevelt, granddaughter of Franklin and Eleanor Roosevelt, daughter of John and Anne Roosevelt, has died as a result of a horseback-riding accident while at Moss Lake Camp in Upstate New York . . ." The news reader confirmed my worst fear as I sat there and now wouldn't shut up. I had no idea what to do or how to feel. I could not speak. Cece immediately offered to take me home. Why would I want to go home? No one was there. Grandmère had left for a hospital in Albany, Haven was probably on his way back from New York, Joanie and her nanny were in Glens Falls, and our kitchen was being redone so there wasn't even a refrigerator. Why should I go home?

I returned to the theater where I retreated into the small ticket booth to hand out reserved tickets and sell the rest. Suddenly, as if a button had been pushed in my brain, I saw the image of Sally's face and started to cry. I could not stop. I wept so hard the tickets I handed out were soggy cardboard mush before reaching the hands of the recipients. After a few minutes, Ron, my kindly coworker, came to my rescue and gently told me I needed to go home. With no car and no one at the theater who could leave during the performance, I called Les, who, after he finished serving dinner to the few guests my grandmother had invited for that weekend, came and drove me home. I sat waiting on the steps to the summer theater, staring at the grass, hardly noticing the few late stragglers rushing past me.

I walked into our house and found Charlie waiting for me. He nodded his head in the direction of Haven's room and said, "Your brother just got back from New York." Without knocking I went into Haven's room and sat on his bed; Haven sat in the overstuffed chair next to the bed. We stared at each other and then we stared at the floor. Finally, Haven broke this numb silence and spoke to the air, "You read about this happening to other people, not to us." I knew what he meant. We had read about people dying, accidents, murders, but they always took place in someone else's family. Now it was our sister. We sat numb, neither of us knew what to do or how to feel. I tried to go upstairs to my room, but Charlie, hearing my sobs, called to me, "Nina, come on down. You won't sleep for now."

I came downstairs and sat next to Charlie. He tried to comfort Haven and me, but we knew he was also shocked and hurting. Around 3:00 in the morning, a car pulled up and our parents came into the dimly lit living room where Haven, Charlie, and I waited, dreading their return, which would make Sally's death a certainty. From the moment I looked at my mother's face, I knew what was expected. Feelings were to be held in check. There would be no public displays of emotion; weeping was to be done privately without disturbing anyone else. I was now certain of my job: support my parents and help them get through the next few weeks without exhibiting my true feelings, which would have been a sign of weakness.

Because my mother knew it would be hard for me to sleep, she handed me a small pill, a striped triangle with bright colors, turquoise on the top, orange in the middle, and crimson red on the bottom. I knew it was one of her sleeping pills. I appreciated her wanting to help me sleep, but I was afraid of the pill. I never took it. Sixty years later I still have that pill.

Early the next morning Grandmère came to our house, and suddenly the phone began to ring; life slammed forward in full motion. Grandmère hugged me and held me tighter and longer than usual. This was her way of communicating that now was not the time for talking about why or even what had happened. While I knew the two of us would talk sometime in the future, now was the time for contacting relatives and friends, and planning a funeral. Joanie and Bea returned from Glens Falls. Joanie was only eight and did not understand what was going on, but she knew something terrible had happened. Grandmère asked my mother and father what she could do to be useful. Having had an ever-present mother-in-law herself, Grandmère had always been careful to respect my parents' privacy and to allow them to make their own decisions. It was no different now, but Grandmère needed to discuss whether or not to cancel her meeting with a presidential candidate scheduled for that weekend at Val-Kill.

John F. Kennedy had won the Democratic Party nomination and was running for president. Even though he knew Grandmère had been a strong supporter of Adlai Stevenson, Mr. Kennedy hoped to gain my grandmother's support for his candidacy. Mr. Kennedy's plan was to meet with Grandmère, accompanied by his political staffers, news reporters, and plenty of photographers to get full advantage of an endorsement from Eleanor Roosevelt. When Mr. Kennedy offered to postpone the meeting, Grandmère wanted to discuss it with my parents before making a decision. They agreed that my grandmother should meet with JFK casually, just the two of them, without the news media. Mr. Kennedy was grateful for the opportunity to go ahead with the meeting. Grandmère's ability, under the stress of a family crisis, to focus on business and maintain her gracious warmth and receive a man whose commitment she questioned (based on his spotty congressional attendance record) continues to amaze me.

The Sunday morning of the planned visit, Aunt Anna and I were in the hallway discussing what to wear to the funeral when Mr. Kennedy and Grandmère emerged from the living room with smiles on their faces. Aunt Anna already knew Mr. Kennedy and greeted him warmly. My grandmother gently and kindly introduced him to me. Mr. Kennedy knew it was my sister who had died, and he gave me a warm smile and a nod of his head which, without words, said, "I'm sorry, but I'm glad to meet you."

I felt naked. For what seemed like the longest time, when I met someone I did not know extremely well, it was awkward and almost painful until the issue of Sally's death was either confronted or, more often, circumvented.

We agreed that Sally should be buried in her favorite dress, a hand-me-down from our cousin Barbara Morgan. It was a sleeveless, full-skirted, red silk dress with a muted pattern—what we called a "party dress." The rest of us scrambled to find something black. Aunt Anna, with whom I had grown close, did not have a black summer dress with her, but she was able to fit into one of mine. In spite of the gravity of the situation, Aunt Anna and I giggled like two school friends as she tried on the two dresses that might be appropriate, neither of which comfortably covered her ample bosom.

My parents had arranged a simple funeral service conducted by Dr. Kidd, the longtime minister of St. James Episcopal Church. I remember the church being packed on that hot summer day, but

I don't remember exactly who came. There was no eulogy, and I only remember an assortment of words. After the service, we followed Sally's casket out of the church to her burial spot, next to Sara Delano Roosevelt, FDR's mother. My mother requested this particular spot because she said, "I know Granny will take care of my Sally." Mummy and Daddy walked down the aisle, following Sally. Haven and I were right behind them, and Grandmère followed us. I saw Mummy reach for Daddy's hand as they walked. Assuming this was a nice thing to do, I grabbed Haven's hand, Haven and I never held hands, and I am sure he thought I was crazy. My parents had decided that Joanie was too young to have to go through a funeral service and left her at home with her nanny. As we reached the door of the church, I could see a crowd of people, at least seventy-five, standing at a respectful distance, under the tall, stately pine trees on the lawn in front of St. James. They waited, quietly, but it felt as if they were staring at us, which made me uncomfortable. I had no idea that people we did not know, who had never met Sally (or any of us), would come to her funeral. Leaving the church, our procession turned left toward the graveyard behind the church.

With only the muted sound of feet crunching on the gravel path, Grandmère, my uncles, their wives, Aunt Anna, her husband Jim, and the rest of the family followed us to the burial site for the last prayers. My parents had requested that the coffin not be lowered into the grave until we had all left. I found the burial site strange and discomforting. There were pretty flowers and fake green grass blankets that hid the newly turned dirt. Dr. Kidd, dressed in his long black robe covered with what looked like a white, lace-bordered tablecloth, opened his prayer book to read his last attempt at consoling words. I felt hollow and greatly relieved when our hot, sweaty family and close friends finally turned to leave Sally in her red dress, carefully hidden in a flower-draped wooden box. The funeral was over.

Grandmère had asked Marge and Les to be in charge of arranging to feed the entire family in our usual style, a casual lunch by the swimming pool. Marge and Les were particularly fond of Sally, as she was fond of them. Sally made sure she sent notes or a postcard to Marge and Les when we were away from Val-Kill. Marge and Les, with help from the rest of our family, carried trays of cold cuts, cheese, potato salad, macaroni salad, iced tea, pound cake, and cookies to a long table set up under the maple tree next to our house. Everyone was still dressed up, but slowly ties were loosened, men's jackets hung on the chairs, shoes came off, and we all tried to laugh . . . at least a little. Grandmère mentioned that Sally would have liked this.

It wasn't until weeks later that I began to piece together how my sister had died. We were told that while riding on Thursday, Sally had gone over a jump, had fallen from her horse but landed on her feet. Assuming there was no serious injury, the staff allowed Sally to continue her regular schedule. Later that night she complained to her cabin counselor of a headache. The counselor gave her a couple of aspirin, but in the morning she still had a headache. While on a morning hike, Sally abruptly sat down on a large rock and put her head between her knees, something we had been taught to do when we felt as if we were about to faint. Sally lost consciousness, toppled off the rock, and was taken by ambulance to a hospital a couple of hours away. Shortly after arriving at the hospital, my sister died. My mother could not bear the thought of having an autopsy performed on her beautiful daughter's delicate body, so the cause of death remains unknown. The assumption at the time was that, when Sally fell from her horse, she cracked or broke her pelvis, which jarred her spinal cord enough to cause a blood clot to form and travel to her brain stem, resulting in her loss of consciousness and eventually her death. With advances in medicine, it is now believed that Sally may have had a genetic heart anomaly that caused momentary loss of oxygen to her brain resulting in her fall from the horse and subsequent death.

At Christmastime, knowing it would be difficult for the family to go through the holiday without Sally, Grandmère took charge and made sure the family rituals were maintained. On special occasions, before the meal, we always proposed a toast,

Figure 9.1. Val-Kill cousins as teenagers, Thanksgiving after Sally's death. Back row: Lauren, Ted, Haven, Stewart; front row: Eleanor, Joan, and Nina. *Source*: personal collection of the author.

first to our country and its leaders, then to those members of the family and friends who were no longer with us. I took this to mean those whom we loved who had died. I was sure this was a silent toast to FDR and long-deceased relatives—and now it included Sally. Grandmère later wrote me, "This Christmas was hard for us all for the loss of Sally was constantly in our minds & hearts, but I find myself thinking of her so often & I realize how much harder it is for all of you. Your Father and Mother have been wonderful but I don't wonder your mother seems less strong to you, it takes time to come back after such a blow—"

Grandmère did not try to impose herself on me or anyone else, but she made certain that we all knew that she was there to share our grief, our loss, and our loneliness. Grandmère had learned to maintain a dignified, stoic exterior while suffering extraordinary loss and sadness in her own life. This may have been a comfort

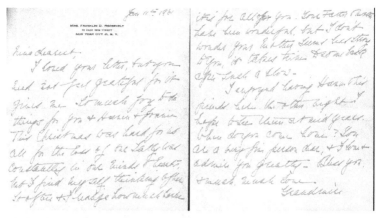

Figure 9.2. Eleanor Roosevelt letter to Nina, January 11, 1961. *Source*: personal collection of the author.

to others, but Grandmère's example led me to think that you were supposed to maintain an outer behavior that did not let others know what you felt like inside. The dead were rarely mentioned for fear that someone else might be hurt by bringing up the loss. This was certainly true in my father's case. We could not mention Sally's name for fear that his emotion would rise to the surface and be seen. This would have embarrassed him and only made him sadder. My siblings and I learned quickly not to mention Sally's name, or my father would become angry as he stifled his emotions. If you did not acknowledge the tears, they were not there. If you did not talk about Sally, she was still at camp. My mother similarly believed showing grief was uncomfortable for others and should be private. Literally, this meant my mother hid her emotion, which in some ways isolated both my parents. "Being strong" in my family meant not letting anyone know how you really felt. I have since learned that it is more helpful to be able to talk about loss and that grieving is an emotion that should be expressed in a manner that brings personal peace.

CHAPTER 10

Closing Doors

November 1962

Figure 10.1. Eleanor Roosevelt's funeral; Franklin Jr., Elliott, Jackie Kennedy, John Kennedy, Lyndon Johnson, Harry Truman, Dwight Eisenhower. *Source*: FDR Library, public domain.

During the summer of 1962, my brother Haven was teaching in the East African nation of Tanzania, then known as Tanganyika; my cousin Chris Roosevelt and I had summer jobs in New York City; my parents and sister Joanie were on a boat trip cruising up the Hudson River, through the northern New York passageway into Lake Champlain; and Grandmère, in between political appearances, was spending as much time as possible in Hyde Park. To support a local New York City candidate, William Fitz Ryan, Grandmère joined a campaign parade, but instead of walking she chose to ride seated in her convertible Fiat Spider with Tubby at the wheel. Normally she would have walked. Chris and I had joined our grandmother for dinner and noticed that she seemed less energetic. We decided to join her for the parade and kept pace jogging beside her car. We watched as she smiled and waved to a crowd that received her with warm enthusiasm. This was one of Grandmère's last public appearances. At Val-Kill Grandmère was different, her usual energy and vitality were rapidly diminishing. Grandmère's shaking hands made pouring the afternoon tea difficult, and you could see the frustration on her tense face. She rarely ventured out for her morning walks, and her engagement in dinner table conversations seemed half-hearted.

On July 28, a few short months before my grandmother would be hospitalized, she held an appreciation party for her longtime friend, Charlie Curnan, presenting him with an engraved silver platter. The Curnans tell a wonderful story about how Charlie was so used to preparing food for parties and helping with whatever was necessary, he never knew the party was in his honor. Even when the gathered guests started singing "For He's a Jolly Good Fellow," Charlie sang along, unaware that they were singing to him. This was my grandmother's last private gathering held at Val-Kill.

That September I headed back to college, at the University of Michigan, without enthusiasm; my world felt different, even tentative. Val-Kill seemed too quiet—a place tense with the realization that our usual level of activity had slowed over the summer and carried an unfamiliar emptiness. Even the frog chorus sounded muted. Goldenrods waved their arms at crows whose caws sent the last songbirds to warmer climates and announced the onset of cold air. The rhythms of Val-Kill were slowing.

When I climbed the well-worn stairs of Val-Kill cottage to say good-bye to my grandmother, I found her sitting in a wicker chair on her sleeping porch, taking in summer's gradual fade into fall's ritual of dying leaves, the smell of wood burning in the fireplace, and early morning ice crystals on blades of grass.

"Will you be home for Thanksgiving, Nina?" Grandmère asked.

"I already have my reservations," I assured her.

"Let me know that you get to Michigan safely, and I do hope the semester goes well," Grandmère said in a soft voice.

"I'll call you when I get there. I plan to work hard and do well this year." I kissed her on the cheek and left her to rest.

In October my mother called to say that, although Grandmère had been hospitalized, she had insisted on being brought home. However, she was not doing well. The family feared that the press would hound the doctors and the family for information if they knew the severity of her illness, so I was sworn to secrecy. I asked my mother if I could come home. "No, Nina, Grandmère won't recognize you. She doesn't recognize most people anymore."

Keeping my promise of secrecy, I floated from class to class in the cold Michigan fall. My thoughts kept wandering back to Val-Kill and my grandmother. It would be years before I recognized that this was the beginning of a downward spiral toward a depression that engulfed me for the next two years. When my mother called on November 7, I knew Grandmère had died. Eleanor Roosevelt was seventy-eight years old and died following what was described as a brief illness, surrounded by family in her New York apartment. I could not imagine my life without Grandmère.

By the time I reached Hyde Park, I was numb. I walked into the living room of Val-Kill cottage, where my grandmother's plain wooden coffin had been placed in front of the fireplace. Pine boughs rested gently on the top; a few green wisps of the long needles caressed the coffin's side. Suddenly my chest tightened, and I could not breathe. I did not want to be in her house. I longed for my brother Haven to give me grounding, but he was still in Africa.

While newspapers worldwide began publishing tributes to the "First Lady of the World," the family, in true Roosevelt spirit, mobilized its efforts to arrange the "simple" funeral service that my grandmother would want but that simultaneously addressed the very real need of security and precise timing for so many dignitaries wishing to pay their respects.

To ensure the safety of President and Mrs. Kennedy, Vice President Johnson, as well as former presidents Eisenhower and Truman, Secret Service officers needed to know the exact schedule for the funeral, the precise route from Val-Kill to the church, and then to the gravesite. It was their job to swarm the Val-Kill property, looking for any areas that needed to be secured. Clearly, the funeral for Eleanor Roosevelt was to be a production, and I distanced myself from my sense of loss by becoming the efficient helper I had been trained to be.

A buffet luncheon at the Stone Cottage was followed by a service at St. James Episcopal Church, with interment in the Rose Garden at Springwood next to FDR. Marge and Les put aside their deeply felt loss and got to work organizing luncheon food for current and former presidents, honored guests, and family who gathered to honor their beloved friend. My mother put me in charge of organizing the cousins to make sure all the guests were served luncheon, observing proper protocol, and ensuring the entire group would be ready to leave for the church within the forty-five minutes allotted for lunch. My cousins, Chris, Stewart, Ted, Lauren, and Eleanor Elliott fell into the same teamwork that we had practiced during the summers of our childhood as we carried out our small contribution to the work at Val-Kill. This time, however, we did not have Haven, the eldest of our work crew, bossing us around. We made certain President Kennedy and the First Lady were served first, then we served the rest of the high-ranking dignitaries in such rapid succession I doubt anyone would have had time to figure out if we applied the proper protocol rules or not. It seemed as if we were dealing plates as quickly as any card shark deals a hand for poker. As soon as a plate was even partially finished, we would remove it from the stunned guest's hands and sweetly ask if we could bring dessert. We served drinks, which included everything from Bloody Marys to coffee and brandy. Chris remembers being complimented by President Kennedy for mixing a perfect drink.

At the appointed time, we all climbed into our assigned black limousines. The long procession drove slowly for the few miles with police escort toward St. James, Hyde Park's small country Episcopal church. Grandmère had once told Charlie Curnan and the Entrups that she could not have done so much of what she did without them. In a gesture of that respect, Grandmère had left instructions that the Curnans and Entrups should be included in the line of limousines carrying family and dignitaries to the church and burial site. My grandmother always treated those around her, regardless of their social status, with the same respect, and in the case of those who worked with and for her at the end of her life, with love. To honor the admiration Grandmère had for the Curnans and the Entrups, Charlie Curnan, Pat Curnan, and Les Entrup were asked to be among those chosen to serve as a pall-bearer for her casket.

Dr. Kidd, our longtime family minister for christenings, weddings, and funerals, led the service. I remember almost nothing about the service except that the church was crowded. Protocol dictated that dignitaries be seated in the front pews which meant that I could not sit in the family pew where I had sat beside Grandmère on so many Sunday mornings. After the appropriate words, the long line of black limousines once again slowly snaked toward Springwood, the Franklin D. Roosevelt Presidential Library and Museum, where a large crowd of people waited in the light rain to get a glimpse of Grandmère's casket, followed by the current and former presidents. With a few prayers and readings from the Bible, the woman who Adlai Stevenson said would rather "light a candle than curse the darkness" was laid to rest.

There would be other memorial services for Eleanor Roosevelt in the months to come. St. John the Divine in New York was filled with mourners paying their respects and honoring her life. Yet I never heard anyone talking about how to continue the values she stood for. My own immaturity conjured up fears that were certainly unreasonable. I feared the fight for civil rights, for equality in health care, access to jobs, and freedom from oppression the world over might not be able to regain the energy to which she had devoted so much of her life.

Grandmère had been the center of my family's life. Gathering for holidays had been because of my grandmother, and now I feared I would lose contact with my aunts, uncles, and cousins. For the first few days after her funeral, my grandmother's death did not seem real. I knew life was sure to change in ways I could not imagine and was surely not prepared to accept. I was also so afraid that everything my grandmother had devoted her life to might be forgotten. Yet, somehow, I knew the changes that were sure to come would be situations I would need to meet as an adult.

CHAPTER 11

Val-Kill in Transition

After Grandmère's death, my father inherited the portion of Val-Kill that he had not already purchased. Father's siblings inherited the contents of the New York apartment and other memorabilia. At this time, 1962, Springwood and the FDR Presidential Library and Museum were part of the National Park Service (NPS) and open to the public. Top Cottage had been sold to a private couple who continued to live there until 2001 when they also sold the home and its surrounding property to the NPS.

Along with the inheritance of Val-Kill came the sole responsibility of the expensive upkeep for the entire estate, including several outbuildings, roads, the land, and of course, the property taxes. With the exception of the time he spent attending boarding school, college, serving in the Navy, and living in California, the Springwood estate and Hyde Park had been Daddy's home. Initially, my parents planned to keep Val-Kill without changes and anticipated that it could one day be taken over by an entity that would preserve it. Fearing the continuing financial drain, my father did investigate the possibility of a government agency conserving the estate and his mother's legacy. Neither the state nor federal government had any interest in preserving her estate as part of the history of the Roosevelt family in the Hudson River Valley. Regardless of her extraordinary contributions to her country and the world, no governmental agency had ever considered honoring a woman in this manner. Father and his siblings donated many of their mother's papers, historical effects, and many personal items to the FDR Presidential Library and Museum to honor their mother's legacy and for the American people to enjoy. No one, however, was interested in her home, which truly reflected the core of Eleanor Roosevelt's spirit.

In 1963, in order to help defray the costs of maintaining Val-Kill, my parents chose to divide Val-Kill Cottage into rental apartments. The former furniture factory was easily divided into smaller apartments, causing little change to the basic layout of the house. By preserving the building's integrity, it could still be taken over by a nonprofit or by a governmental agency and turned into a place for people to learn more about how Eleanor Roosevelt lived. This solution appeared to work well, and the property continued to be well cared for—for a time.

While the property looked as if nothing had changed, the vitality of Val-Kill had been rapidly transformed, and to me the future felt like negotiating a fog of pea soup. Our routines continued—my parents lived during the week in their New York apartment, spending weekends at Val-Kill. Daddy still went to his job on Wall Street and played golf on Saturdays. Mummy continued her routine with friends in the city and reading or gardening at Val-Kill.

The sadness of Sally's loss engulfed our family in an unacknowledged dark cloud. Sally's life and death remained unspoken, her name not mentioned, yet the repressed thoughts, questions, and feelings were not erased from our minds and affected our interactions with each other. This was especially true with my father, who had a special relationship with Sally, due in large part to the time of her birth. Sally, our parents' third child, was born after the war, when Daddy was no longer deployed by the Navy. By this time, he had settled into a job in Los Angeles and was now able to enjoy being a father. Sally had an engaging personality—she loved animals, especially horses, and made friends easily. Although undiagnosed, Sally exhibited symptoms of a learning disability, which made school difficult for her. Sally, like so many teens, began to feel as if she did not fit in with our parents and began to distance herself from them. Certainly, they would have accepted this as part of her growing up. However, to lose their daughter during this developmental stage must have made her loss especially devastating.

Two years after Sally's death and with Grandmère's health declining, Val-Kill began to feel lonely, as if a pall had been cast over the family and all who were connected with life at Val-Kill. With Grandmère's death, there was no longer a center of the Roosevelt family. Charlie and his wife, Millie, continued to work for my father, but Marge and Les took a short-lived job with Uncle Elliott in Florida. We no longer enjoyed picnics, meals were quiet, holiday gatherings shrunk from thirty people to five and did not include other friends and family who had been such a constant presence at Val-Kill because of Grandmère.

Compounded by the death of Grandmère so soon after the loss of Sally, the structure of our immediate family began to deteriorate. Communication was stilted and formal—none of us were able to express what we were feeling. Instead, in the tradition of both sides of our family, we tried to ignore our thoughts and feelings and pretended to act as if nothing had changed. My siblings and I learned not to mention Sally's name or our father would become angry as he stifled his emotions. The passage of time had not allowed either of my parents to adjust to the devastating death of their vibrant, young daughter Sally. The doctor's explanation to my parents was vague at best. We were told that a fall from her horse caused a blood clot in her brain that resulted in death. With so much unacknowledged grief after two significant deaths, it was sad to realize that my parents did not know how to find solace in each other.

I had not realized until after Grandmère died how important she was in the life of my father, John. The youngest of the five children, he was the most reserved, the most stable personally and professionally, and was the only one, as long as she was alive, who had not gone through a divorce.

Figure 11.1. FDR and Eleanor Roosevelt's children: Franklin Jr., John, Anna, James, Elliott. *Source*: Photo by Jay Te Winburn, public domain.

It became clear to me that my grandmother was the anchor of Daddy's life, and with the loss of his mother, he was now adrift. Between 1962 and 1965 many of his actions seemed inexplicable. Our animals, when Haven and I were not home, were neglected. Daddy did not notice or appear to care how much he drank. At times he seemed to enjoy driving recklessly. Most noticeable was his withdrawal from any interest in his children's lives. Daddy had not been particularly present in my life, but now he was disappearing not only from me but from my mother and siblings as well.

Several months after our grandmother's death, my brother Haven returned from teaching in Africa and was attending law school. Following Grandmère's funeral, I went back to the University of Michigan. During the early part of the fall semester, I had not managed to feel a part of either the university's activities or opportunities. Now with the onset of ice and snow, I felt it was just a matter of time before I would be one of the last leaves to fall and be carried off by the cold Ann Arbor winter wind. There was no doubt I was floundering and felt alone. I remember attending classes but not really listening to the lectures, nothing seemed to sink in. After class, on my way back to my dorm, I passed a small church that I went into just to sit in the quiet, to escape. My grades started to drop, and I isolated myself from friends and activities. There was a distinct possibility that I was about to flunk out of college. I decided to return to New York at the end of the fall term and enrolled at the New School for Social Research. I was determined to complete my undergraduate degree. Forced by the format of most of my classes, which were seminars requiring oral participation, I began to engage. The focus on discussion and research helped me to regain my sense of purpose. Neither of my parents understood why I had left Michigan, nor did they ask. Their own suffering and conflict in their marriage at this time precluded their ability to move beyond trying to stabilize their own lives.

When I was with my parents, I observed that my father's eyes looked as if he were confused. There were times his gaze was so far away, I was not sure he knew who I was. He appeared to be looking for something he would never find. Before dinner Daddy drank his martinis, sat through dinner with few words, and after dinner, with a demitasse of coffee beside his chair in the living room, fell asleep, snoring loudly. On weekends, my father sat with his morning coffee, the New York Times open and held in front of his face. He looked as if he were hiding from the day. When any of us joined him, while we ate breakfast, he was silent, unable to acknowledge that we were there. I still have an image of my father with his face covered and his long legs protruding beneath the opened newspaper, as if he did not want to be seen.

My mother compensated by spending more time with her friends. Nearly every day she lunched with a friend and then went shopping. At night, my mother stayed up, drinking scotch until the wee hours of the morning. She then slept late in the morning, getting up after my father had gone to work or off to play golf. They participated together in the usual family rituals such as Thanksgiving and Christmas, but it was clear that my parents were less and less interested in spending time together.

The deaths of two family members within a very short time seemed to push each of my parents into depression. I did not know how to help and had to watch as my mother continued to take her "sleeping pills" and my father detach himself from our lives. Since neither would ever think of seeking the help of a professional, no formal diagnosis could be made. They each tried to reestablish some semblance of a normal life, but haunted by their own sadness, they became more and more distant from their former selves and one another—and their children.

By the time Joan was ten, our family was well on the way to disintegrating. Haven and I were beginning our own lives and were spending less time at Val-Kill. While I was still living in New York, I did try to go to Val-Kill as much as possible to spend time with Joan. The gap of ten years between Joan and me made her life seem more like that of an only child. Neither of our parents had ever been interested in activities that were child-centered, preferring that we chose our own activities and entertain ourselves. Fortunately for Joan, mother had a close friend, Sandy Coburn, who was a widow with two daughters. Sandy's youngest daughter, Wendy, became Joanie's close friend from the age of eight. The two girls loved horses as well as each other's company. Their bond was such that Wendy, after Sally's death, was included as if she were a sister of Joanie's. To the delight of the girls, their friendship allowed my parents to include Wendy for the weekends at Val-Kill. The two girls typically left the house early in the morning and spent the day at a nearby riding stable. Joan loved being with Wendy, and when they weren't riding, they enjoyed the freedom of being at Val-Kill. Even though our grandmother was no longer there, Joan and Wendy began to develop their own rhythm with friends from the stables, and both thought of the place as their home, even if they were only there on weekends.

The pattern of my parents' life, by the spring of 1964, appeared to have established some sort of equilibrium. Haven was in his last year of law school. In June I was graduating from college and was getting married. My marriage took place in St. James, the church in Hyde Park my family had attended for generations and where I had attended with Grandmère. This was the only time I did not respect my parents unspoken wishes that we ignore the loss of Sally. She would have been my maid of honor, and somehow I wanted to include her in this important occasion. At the conclusion of the church service, I walked out of the church and, instead of getting into the waiting limousine, took most of the flowers from my wedding bouquet and went to the back of the church to place the flowers on Sally's grave. It wasn't a part of the wedding plan, but I missed my sister. My mother's face showed her disapproval, and my father, standing next to her, continued to stare stone-faced as they waited for me to get into the car that would lead the way back to the Stone Cottage for the reception. On this occasion, Aunt Anna and all three of my uncles had returned to Val-Kill to join in the festivities. This was the first time they had all been together at Val-Kill since their mother's funeral. I was especially glad that Aunt Anna had come, as I had grown close to her over the years. Sadly, with more than two hundred people, there was little time to spend with anyone in particular.

After the wedding, my mother and Wendy's mother planned to take their young daughters to Norway for a few weeks in July and August. What none of us had any clue about was that, while my mother was away, my father moved to end their marriage. Toward the end of their stay in Norway, my mother received a letter from my father telling her that he wanted a divorce. At first Mummy believed she could reason with my father, and they could somehow save their marriage of twenty-six years. All attempts at discussion and protestations with my father, however, fell on deaf ears. Mother could not face the reality of being alone as she aged, and I believe she continued to love my father. She was deeply hurt and angry; her pride had suffered a massive blow.

With the knowledge of an impending divorce, we soon learned that Daddy had become involved with a woman who was able to control Daddy's decisions and occupy all his time and affection. Negotiations for my parents' divorce took a few months. My mother agreed to avoid the American courts and go to Mexico for their divorce. Within hours of the divorce being granted, my father was married to our now stepmother, Irene, and they left aboard the Cunard Line for a European honeymoon.

It was soon apparent that our stepmother had different ideas about how Stone Cottage should look and who could visit. She made it clear that children were not welcome in what was now her house. Even the help, who had taken care of the cleaning, cooking, laundry, and general household maintenance, faced the dramatic change in attitude. When the towels were not fluffy enough, the laundress was berated; if anything was left out of place, Joanie and Wendy were reprimanded; the food Millie prepared was never up to the standards set by Irene; even the furniture was not to her liking. Charlie suddenly was told to keep the grounds looking like a freshly groomed poodle.

Wendy and Joan spent their weekends at Val-Kill avoiding confrontations with Irene by going to the stables, riding, and hanging out with their friends. During the week, Joan lived with our mother in an apartment in the city. Unable to figure out how to manage her own life changes, our mother had difficulty focusing her attention on her youngest daughter's needs. Haven was now married and beginning his law career. I was living and working in Virginia while my husband began his career. This meant Joan was alone to negotiate the changing family dynamics. School became especially difficult for Joan, and after a couple of years of falling behind academically, the school suggested that summer school might help so that she would not have to repeat a grade. Neither of our parents were able to deal with how to handle a summer program for Joan. My mother called me to ask if I could enroll Joanie in a summer program near me and have her live with me for the summer. By this time, I had moved to Ohio and had two small boys. I embraced the idea of having

Joan live with us for the summer and hoped by doing so, we could provide the support she needed. Joan actually enjoyed her classes, and she was proud of her ability to earn excellent grades, which allowed her to participate in her eighth-grade graduation with her classmates. As a reward I took her riding whenever she was not in school or doing homework. Joan had a good summer, although she may not have appreciated her older sister acting like her mother and making sure she not only kept up with school but helped around the house as well.

Joan was then sent to a boarding school on Long Island for high school. Fortunately, she made friends and felt at home there. She continued riding and thrived under the coaching of Harry de Leyer, a noted equestrian and owner/trainer of the famous show jumper, Snowman.

I was not welcome to visit Val-Kill with my small children, who might be disruptive. I did manage to get permission in the summer of 1968 to take my young son, Haven, named after my brother, to Val-Kill while my father and stepmother were away. I wanted to introduce him to Charlie and to show my son the place I had loved while growing up. Charlie, acting as a surrogate grandfather, seemed delighted to play with him. Haven was given an ice cream cone that of course melted all over both Charlie and himself. Charlie appeared happy to be able to play with this next generation of the family. I loved watching them, and it made me feel as if some of the cherished parts of Val-Kill could never be entirely taken away.

Eventually, the economic drain of Val-Kill and spending her weekends away from New York City was enough for Irene to begin planning for a different lifestyle. Val-Kill would have been more acceptable to her if it were located in a socially prominent place, like Newport or the Hamptons on Long Island. My brother, sister, and I were never told what the plan for Val-Kill was. We did learn, thirdhand, that Roosevelt memorabilia and Val-Kill furniture were being sold at an auction in preparation for selling all of the Val-Kill property. On a bright Saturday morning in the fall of 1970, Haven, Joan, and I gathered unannounced on the lawn in front of the Stone Cottage to try to purchase some of the items being sold. Some of these items belonged to us. It surprised both my father and stepmother that we were there. They had tried to keep us from knowing about the items being sold. We were not given the opportunity to remove the few pieces of furniture, books, and wall hangings that had been given to us by our grandmother and which we left for safe-keeping until we were settled in homes of our own. The Val-Kill we had known and loved was now gone.

We learned that the prospective buyers had plans to turn the entire Val-Kill estate into a housing development. Zoning issues, however, became a stumbling block for their envisioned real estate project. Local residents protested any rezoning, and further destruction to the property was delayed.

Val-Kill remained full of cherished memories, but we were establishing roots elsewhere. With the sale of Val-Kill, my father and stepmother continued to live in their New York apartment. Grandchildren were definitely not permitted in the apartment for fear that they would either spill something or make a mess. Since I did not live in the city, my only contact with my father was over the phone. Occasionally, if I came to New York, I would meet him for lunch at a restaurant.

For a few years after their divorce, my mother lived in an apartment in New York, where her children and grandchildren were welcome as long as we did not rely on her for babysitting. As soon as Joanie finished school, however, Mother decided she no longer wanted to live in New York and moved to Majorca, Spain, where her friend and former sister-in-law, Faye Emerson, was living. Not long after her move, Mother and her sister Sally were in London visiting friends and family. Aunt Sally and my mother planned to leave London on the same day, returning to their respective countries. Aunt Sally left on an early morning flight for Hawaii, and Mother planned an afternoon flight back to Majorca. I got a call from my brother telling me that our mother had suffered a stroke and never made it to the airport. She had been found on the floor of her hotel room by the hotel manager, who let my brother know that he had arranged for her to be taken to a nearby hospital. Two days later I flew to London to assess Mummy's medical condition and begin the process of deciding what the next steps would be.

Before allowing me to go into my mother's hospital room, the nurse took me aside and warned me that my mother could not walk, had limited control of her arms, could only utter a few unrecognizable sounds, and had trouble eating. Upon entering the room, I saw my mother, unmoving, and a mere wisp of what she had once been. The nurse said, "Mrs. Roosevelt, you have a lovely daughter who is here to visit you."

The nurse was surprised when my mother replied, with clarity, "And she's nice too."

That was the nicest thing my mother had ever said about me, at least in front of me. Even though I choked up with tears, I knew something of my mother was still there behind her feeble body. Fearing how much time I would have to spend away from her bedside while I made arrangements to bring my mother back to the United States, I contacted my Aunt Sally, who agreed to turn around and take the next flight back to London. While Aunt Sally stayed with my mother, I spent most of every day making all the proper arrangements to find a commercial airline that would be willing to take a person, on a stretcher, to New York. Securing the proper medical and government approvals also took time and a great deal of paperwork. Eventually, I managed to get an airline that had a plane going to New York with few passengers aboard, to accommodate my mother. Haven had made all the arrangements so that upon our arrival in New York, we were met on the tarmac by an ambulance that took her directly to St. Luke's Hospital. Once mother was settled at St. Luke's, Haven and I began assessing how to arrange for the sort of care she would need and what her future might be. Within a couple of days, however, as her doctor expected, mother had a second stroke. Her three children were by her side when she slipped away.

By the time our mother died, Joanie had graduated from college and was living and working in the Hudson River Valley, where she was married and raising a daughter. Always interested in horses, Joan and a friend opened a stable where they trained and boarded horses. Joan rarely saw Daddy but was fortunate enough to spend a good deal of time with our Uncle Franklin, who had a farm nearby.

At this time, Haven was living with his wife and four daughters, in Chappaqua, New York, and was busy with his legal career. My brother was in the city daily during the week and tried to keep in touch with our father, but other than an occasional lunch, he never managed to breach the distance that was now entrenched.

In 1975, while I was living in Ohio, my own marriage ended in divorce. In 1978 I remarried and completed my graduate studies in psychology a few years later. With our three children, my husband and I moved to Arizona in 1988 for my husband to continue his biophysics, and later neuroscience, research. In Arizona I worked in the public sector, with adults and children whose families had suffered the ravages of drug addiction and mental illness.

Retirement from Bache and Co. left my father with time on his hands and no particular interests. The question of retirement brought an angry response—"I am not retiring, I am still working." Although no apparent job was on the horizon, Daddy was sure he could step into a position at one of the University of New York campuses. John Roosevelt was shy—he had been trained to hide his true feelings and never talked about the things that impacted his life, such as his war experiences, the death of his parents, his childhood, the death of his daughter, a failed marriage, and a new marriage. It is no wonder that Daddy had difficulty adjusting and appeared to lose his way. Aunt Anna told me my father was not happy with his second marriage and had, in fact, discussed divorce with his sister and brother-in-law. It was Aunt Anna's assessment that, once he and Irene married, she made all the decisions within the marriage, and my father lost the strength to do anything except follow along without enthusiasm. It seemed as if he lost the strength to make any changes and just gave up. In 1981 Daddy was diagnosed with heart disease and died after a short illness.

Epilogue

Val-Kill Today

Val-Kill was the only place Eleanor Roosevelt truly felt was her home. An invitation from this very public person to Val-Kill allowed visitors, friends, and family to share the restorative qualities of this rustic setting. This was the place where my grandmother, away from public scrutiny, could relax. There was never a difference between the way my grandmother acted in private, with family and friends, and the way she acted with reporters and cameras recording her every move. Eleanor Roosevelt, First Lady of the World, consistently acted in accordance with the values and beliefs she spoke about throughout her life. Val-Kill was the place for her to relax, reflect, have fun, and renew her spirits. Even now, to visit Val-Kill is to begin to understand who Eleanor Roosevelt was and the values she embodied.

She had lived in many houses: Springwood, which belonged to her mother-in-law; Campobello, which was only for a couple of months in the summer; the White House, which belonged to the American people; and temporary residences with FDR as they moved between New York City, Albany, and Washington, D.C. Val-Kill, however, was the place she built and that reflected her character. Grandmère did not have to share the house with her husband, who did enjoy swimming in the pool, nor with her children. Out of the public eye, she was free to invite anyone she wanted to visit. Photographs of friends and family hung like patterned wallpaper—a pattern that was periodically rotated, as there were so many photographs of her large family. Books jammed every bookshelf. Memorabilia, mostly from her trips, covered every available flat surface in the house. Interior decorators were not consulted when my grandmother chose furniture for Val-Kill. Comfort and simplicity were the only guiding principles for furnishing the many rooms in this rambling former factory. Nearly all of the wooden furniture, tables, chairs, bureaus, desks, and mirrors had been made in this building before it was converted into her home. Pewter wall sconces and bedspreads, crafted by the men and women who were part of Val-Kill Industries could be seen throughout the house. None of the rooms were formal, and all of them affirmed the warmth for which Eleanor Roosevelt was known.

One of the reasons I wrote this book is to honor the Curnans, the Entrups, and all the other loyal people who have contributed to our family, and my grandmother in particular, to make Val-Kill what it was. All of the valuable behind-the-scenes work was carried out with professionalism and was fueled by their personal commitment to a woman whom they loved, and who, in return, loved and respected them. Without their dedication my grandmother may not have been able to live her life as fully as she had. The relationship between Grandmère and her staff taught me that every individual is to be respected and valued for their contributions. All who either visited or worked at Val-Kill, from the most powerful to the most humble, enjoyed the warm hospitality of a household that respected their humanity and diverse backgrounds.

Val-Kill and my grandmother were a part of the community of Hyde Park and the Hudson River Valley. Many people from the area had joined Grandmère for picnics, had enjoyed dinners and holiday celebrations held at Val-Kill. It was the men and women of the Hudson River Valley who truly appreciated their famous neighbor and understood that she wanted to be treated without any fuss. Grandmère was able to go to church or to the grocery store without a whirl of people asking for an autograph. There was always a friendly greeting, common in any town where most people know each other.

After my grandmother's death, there was a natural concern about what would happen to the property and the historic home of their beloved neighbor. Hyde Park was growing rapidly, and there was a fear that the property would be turned into another housing development. Soon after Val-Kill was sold for potential development, a grassroots effort was launched to keep this historic property intact and to honor the life and work of Eleanor Roosevelt. The first battle to protest any zoning changes that would include Val-Kill seemed to have discouraged the developers who owned the property at the time. After years with no definitive plan for the Val-Kill property, the owners knew development was not feasible and agreed to negotiate with the government's interest in protecting the house and surrounding property.

In 1975 the Hyde Park Visual Environment Committee (HPVEC) and the office of the New York State Lieutenant Governor's Office joined forces to acquire Val-Kill. The idea was that it would eventually become a museum or, at the very least, a place for small conferences that would honor Eleanor Roosevelt. Eleanor Roosevelt's Val-Kill, Inc. was formed by this coalition. The committee, headed by Joyce Ghee (HPVEC) and Nancy Dubner (Lt. Governor's Office), included several other dedicated men and women from the Hudson River Valley. Margaret Zamierowski, the committee's first volunteer, worked diligently to organize and administer the activities designed to encourage others to join the effort to establish Val-Kill as a permanent part of the history of the Hudson River Valley. Mrs. Zamierowski later joined the board and devoted most of her time to honoring the legacy of Eleanor Roosevelt.

In response to their grassroots work, New York's senators, Jacob Javits and Daniel Moynihan, introduced a bill in Congress to authorize the establishment of the Eleanor Roosevelt National Historic Site. At the time it was unusual to expect that a piece of legislation honoring a woman, particularly one who had never held elective office, could pass. However, this was a woman who was admired not just in the United States but throughout the world for her contributions as First Lady, her work at the United Nations, which led to acceptance of the Universal Declaration of Human Rights, and her many fights against social injustice at home and abroad. With constant lobbying, dedication, and hard work from family members and the people of the Hudson River Valley, and the strong congressional support of Representative Claude Pepper (D-FL), Senate Bill 1125 was passed by the 95th Congress. In May 1977 President Carter signed the bill establishing the Eleanor Roosevelt National Historic Site "to commemorate . . . the life and work of an outstanding woman in American History."

The legislation charged the National Park Service (NPS) with the significant task of purchasing and refurbishing Val-Kill with as many items that had been there during the time my grandmother lived there as were obtainable. Work still continues to bring back many of the photographs that hung on the walls, as well as the memorabilia that was on display and part of Val-Kill. In addition, the NPS has done a tremendous amount of work on the grounds, which had not been cared for in years. The gardens are being restored, and the outbuildings are being used to show a video and explain the history of Val-Kill. Today, Val-Kill looks almost as though my grandmother never left, if perhaps a bit more manicured. It is a joy to see people jogging up the long driveway, strolling around the grounds, and enjoying all the things my grandmother also loved. The house feels as if Mrs. Roosevelt just stepped out for one of her trips but will soon return.

The legislation also placed significant importance on continuing the legacy of Eleanor Roosevelt through programming. An agreement was signed between the NPS and the local group, Eleanor Roosevelt's Val-Kill, Inc., a private nonprofit, to implement onsite and outreach programs honoring Eleanor Roosevelt's legacy. The congressional legislation, however, did not include funding for the education/legacy work at Val-Kill. Without funding for the continuation of teaching about Eleanor Roosevelt's life, these programs rely on the generosity of funders who also want the spirit of the Declaration of Human Rights, social justice, civil rights, and moral leadership to be brought to young people from all over the world. Even though the name of the organization, now called the Eleanor Roosevelt Center at Val-Kill (ERVK), changed over time, the work continues to promote continuing education and seminars relating to the humanitarian, social justice, and civil rights issues to which Eleanor Roosevelt devoted her life.

Val-Kill today is a living memorial to Eleanor's considerable intellect and is a means for carrying forward her interests and concerns through education and leadership programs emanating from the site. For more than twenty years, the Girl's Leadership Worldwide (GLW) program has brought young women from all over the world to Val-Kill to bring their leadership potential to life. Based on the model of Eleanor Roosevelt's leadership, these girls engage in activities to learn about citizenship, social justice, human rights, and socially conscious leadership within their own communities and the world. One of the graduates I came to know from this program came from an abusive patriarchal culture and realized that women did not have to be treated the way they were in her community. Steadfastly, this young woman gathered her courage and against all odds made the choice to change her life. She applied for and was granted sanctuary in the United States, found work and housing, perfected her English, learned to drive, and is continuing her higher education. In an essay for one of her college courses, she wrote, "Being a truly inspiring and influential leader, Mrs. Roosevelt has inspired many young girls today who find courage and hope by learning about Roosevelt's work and attending workshops at the Eleanor Roosevelt Center at Val-Kill in Hyde Park, New York." I know my grandmother would be so proud of all the young women who have begun to understand that their voice matters and are able to believe in their own courage and abilities as they continue learning and accepting the responsibilities of citizenship.

Launched in 2013, the Eleanor Roosevelt Community College Emerging Leaders program (ECCEL) for men and women prepares students to lead in all aspects of their lives. The focus is on self-discovery, skill development, experiential learning, and global citizenship. Many of these students have reported that the experiences offered through this program helped them focus on a future they may never have envisioned for themselves.

A few years ago, a woman told me how her mother, during World War II, left alone with three children while her farmer husband was fighting abroad, was forced to keep the farm going to feed the family. Every morning at dawn, her mother went outside and said, "Please, Eleanor Roosevelt, tell me what would you do today to get through?" The name Eleanor Roosevelt was not to be spoken in their house, but her mother disregarded the taboo. She knew she needed extra guidance and called to my grandmother. ERVK's programs offer the values of Eleanor Roosevelt that give us strength to face what may seem impossible.

In addition to these programs, ERVK partners with other organizations to promote the teaching and implementation of the Universal Declaration of Human Rights. ERVK, founded in the spirit and name of Eleanor Roosevelt, continues to provide programs and activities that not only support the legacy of Eleanor Roosevelt but helps young people in particular to be inspired to carry forward, in their own way, the idea that human rights begin at home in our own communities.

ERVK's partnership with the National Park Service and their stewardship of the Eleanor Roosevelt National Historic Site brings the work of furthering Eleanor's legacy to life. Their interpretation of Eleanor's life, and time at Val-kill, creates an experience for each of us to connect to her intellectually and emotionally and take action through support of one of the Center's programs and initiatives.

During my grandmother's life, Val-Kill was a center of diversity, a respite for a weary world traveler, and a family home. Without the selfless devotion of the staff, who became friends, my grandmother's activities and outreach would have been curtailed. To me, Val-Kill is an example of the way my grandmother lived what she preached. The world continues to honor this extraordinary woman for all her accomplishments and the legacy she has left behind. Understanding who she was when she was at home, traveling, and interacting with friends and family also reminds us that she was a genuine person who truly cared about what she believed were inequities throughout the world. Because of her values and desire for the well-being of others, Eleanor Roosevelt has become a beacon for so many around the world.

From an early age, the time I spent with my grandmother introduced me to her energy, focused interest, and compassion. Not only is her life a model that gave a voice and dignity to people struggling with poverty and hopelessness, but it is an exemplar for all of us as we negotiate our lives. Her experiences taught her to figure out ways to bring strength to individuals who would in turn strengthen America and contribute to more peace in the world. My grandmother overcame her own shyness and continued to grow and learn throughout her life. She was a true listener and had the ability to leave her own ego behind when negotiating solutions to complicated problems.

Since Grandmère's death, I still feel her guidance and realize how important she was to me as I negotiated both the joys and challenges of my own life. Fortunately, my grandmother encouraged me and so many others to live our lives with honesty, dignity, and respect for others. She encouraged us to nurture our own talents and advised us to be aware that we are part of a world with diverse foundations, experiences, and ideas. We may express our beliefs in unfamiliar ways. We may live our everyday lives with different traditions, but we must continue to work together to help each other realize the dignity of each of our lives. Grandmère reminded me that, wherever I was, whatever I was doing, or whomever I was talking to, I could always learn something. Grandmère taught me to absorb as much as I could from whatever situation I found myself in.

Grandmère felt it was our individual responsibility to work toward equality and humanitarianism for all. During a speech to a group of newly arrived immigrants in New York, Grandmère, with strength in her voice, told the audience that it was their responsibility as newcomers to work in their neighborhoods promoting the ideals of democracy and the values of their new country. Stella Hershon, who had escaped the Nazi takeover of Austria, was in that audience and later wrote about how much Eleanor Roosevelt had influenced her life as an immigrant in this country. Stella carried those words with her and built a life around taking responsibility to contribute to a stronger democracy. Through her writing, Stella brought the horrors of Nazism to her readers. Few political initiatives in New York were not studied and commented on as Stella became a vocal community member.

When I came to live at Val-Kill, I had no idea how the next twelve years spent with my grandmother would impact my life. My introduction to people who worked with us to make Val-Kill a place for a former First Lady and a force, in her own right, for those less fortunate the world over, gave me the foundation to live my life believing in working together with respect and caring. In looking back over my time with Grandmère, I marvel at all the ways she improved the lives of others with her activism and her example. But to me, she is my loving grandmother, whose warm embrace consoled me at the worst of times, who entrusted me with a priceless gift when I was on the cusp of adulthood, and who tucked me in at night with a kiss and the touch of her so-soft cheek when I was still just a nervous seven-year-old girl.

Index

Page numbers in *italics* indicate illustrations.